To Make Beautiful the Capitol

Rediscovering the Art of Constantino Brumidi

UNITED
STATES
SENATE

To Make Beautiful the Capitol

Rediscovering the Art of Constantino Brumidi

Compiled by
Amy Elizabeth Burton

Prepared under the direction of the
U.S. Senate Commission on Art

U.S. GOVERNMENT PRINTING OFFICE
WASHINGTON, D.C.: 2014

113th Congress, 2nd Session   S. Pub 113–10
Printed pursuant to 2 USC 2102(a)

U.S. Senate Commission on Art

Chairman:
Harry Reid, Nevada

Vice Chairman:
Mitch McConnell, Kentucky

Patrick J. Leahy, Vermont
Charles E. Schumer, New York
Pat Roberts, Kansas

Executive Secretary:
Nancy Erickson

Curator:
Diane K. Skvarla

Works of art illustrated are by Constantino Brumidi unless otherwise noted. Illustrations are from the records of the Office of Senate Curator except where other collection or photography credits are provided.

Principal photography by James Rosenthal, courtesy of the Architect of the Capitol. Photography credits appear on pages 130–31. Images have been used with the consent of their respective owners.

Printed and bound in the United States of America.

        Library of Congress Cataloging-in-Publication Data

 To make beautiful the Capitol : rediscovering the art of Constantino Brumidi / compiled by Amy Elizabeth Burton. –
– 1st [edition].
        pages cm
Includes bibliographical references.
"Prepared under the direction of the U.S. Senate Commission on Art."
1. Brumidi, Constantino, 1805–1880--Criticism and interpretation. 2. United States Capitol (Washington, D.C.)
3. Mural painting and decoration, American--Washington (D.C.)--19th century. 4. Mural painting and decoration--
Conservation and restoration—Washington (D.C.) I. Burton, Amy Elizabeth. II. Cunningham–Adams, Christiana. III.
Skvarla, Diane K., 1957- IV. Wolanin, Barbara A. (Barbara Ann) V. Ritchie, Donald A., 1945- Engineer and the
artist. VI. United States. Congress. Senate. Commission on Art.
 ND237.B877T6 2013
 759.13--dc23
                        2013362000

Cover: Eagle and garland of flowers, Brumidi Corridors (Patent Corridor). Architect of the Capitol.

Frontispiece: Patriotic shield, Brumidi Corridors (West Corridor).

Pages viii–ix: Brumidi Corridors (North and West Corridors). Architect of the Capitol.

Contents

" I have no longer any desire for fame or fortune. My one ambition and my daily prayer is that I may live long enough to make beautiful the Capitol of the one country on earth in which there is liberty. "

Brumidi

Foreword

It has been my great privilege to work at the United States Capitol for 20 years, and in my current position, to be involved with the preservation and protection of the Senate's art. When I first arrived, I noticed that the Senate wing had been altered by the ever-evolving needs of a working public building. Office equipment and phone booths intruded on the historic interiors, while heavy layers of overpaint from numerous early, misguided restoration efforts obscured the true nature of Constantino Brumidi's beautiful 19th-century murals. Nevertheless, Brumidi's art instilled in me a sense of awe and purpose that reflects the important legislative work performed in the Capitol. Over the years, painstaking restoration has gradually transformed the flat, dull, altered murals into the exquisitely modeled originals with their bright and delicate colors. Watching this transformation, I came to recognize the Capitol as more than just a building; it is a canvas upon which the story of this nation is told. Today, with all those who work in the Capitol and who serve in the United States Senate, I share a deep sense of pride in Brumidi's efforts "to make beautiful" the Capitol. Brumidi's art is truly a tribute to our nation and a lasting heritage for America. As executive secretary to the U.S. Senate Commission on Art and as secretary of the Senate, I am pleased to present *To Make Beautiful the Capitol: Rediscovering the Art of Constantino Brumidi.*

THE HONORABLE NANCY ERICKSON
Secretary of the Senate and Executive Secretary
to the Senate Commission on Art

Opposite: **Eagle, Brumidi Corridors (detail, Patent Corridor).**

Introduction

Over a span of 25 years, Constantino Brumidi (1805–1880) decorated the walls and ceilings of the United States Capitol in a manner befitting a great public building. In the Senate wing, he designed and painted murals, some in the traditional fresco medium, for important spaces such as the President's Room, the Senate Reception Room, and the renowned Brumidi Corridors—the august hallways that today bear the artist's name. Brumidi's monumental fresco in the Capitol Rotunda, *The Apotheosis of Washington*, covers an impressive 4,664 square feet and yet took just 11 months to complete. His prodigious efforts at the Capitol were truly a labor of love. When Brumidi died in February of 1880, *The Washington Post* reflected: "He was the genius of the Capitol. So many of its stateliest rooms bear the touch of his tireless brush that he shall always be associated with it."[1]

Opposite: **Plenty, detail from *Liberty, Peace, Plenty, War,* oil on canvas sketch, ca. 1858.**

Brumidi accepted his first assignment for the Capitol in December of 1854, when he was a mature 49 years of age. Having emigrated from Italy just two years earlier, the Italian-born artist arrived in Washington, D.C., as construction progressed on the Capitol extension, which comprised the Senate and House wings. Shortly thereafter, in March of 1855, a new cast-iron dome for the building was authorized. Brumidi possessed the skills, temperament, and motivation to take on the demanding challenge of designing and painting historical frescoes and decorative murals for the building's new interiors. He became a naturalized U.S. citizen in 1857, and in later years, was something of a fixture at the Capitol. Members of the press and visitors to the building often observed "Signor Brumidi" at work and engaged the amiable artist in conversation about the subjects of his paintings.

During the two and a half decades that Brumidi ornamented the Capitol with his "tireless brush," he worked through 6 presidents' terms and 13 Congresses, and the young nation grew from 31 to 38 states. Changes in administration, controversies about his decorative style, the turmoil of the Civil War, and his own advancing age did not deter him from his life's work. Brumidi's son Laurence reflected on his father's efforts: "All labor was given freely out of pride in the Capitol Building of the United States and love for the land of his adoption." [2]

After Brumidi's death, his murals were altered by artists hired to repair and restore the paintings in the era before modern conservation. These alterations managed only to diminish Brumidi's originals, in many cases quite severely, and his reputation suffered accordingly. In recent decades, Brumidi's artistic contribution to the Capitol has become a subject of serious study for scholars and a primary occupation for fine art conservators. Starting in the 1980s, Congress supported an extensive and long-term conservation program to restore Brumidi's work in the Capitol. As a result of a decade of researching Brumidi's life and of managing the mural conservation program, Architect of the Capitol Curator Barbara A. Wolanin published *Constantino Brumidi: Artist of the Capitol* in 1998. This book discusses Brumidi's background and painting techniques, as well as the political context in which the artist worked at the Capitol; the book also highlights the conservation and restoration efforts that had been accomplished by the mid-1990s.

Since then, the mural conservation program has made sweeping changes to the appearance of the Senate wing of the Capitol and has allowed a fresh examination of Brumidi's artwork. These changes are most evident in the Brumidi Corridors, where the reemergence of the historical detail in Brumidi's original murals has opened doors for new research, discoveries, and interpretations. What we know about the artist has been enhanced by the addition of several of Brumidi's preliminary sketches to the Senate collection and by the transcription of a key journal detailing the building of the Capitol extension, as well as by recently digitized resources that point to the inspiration for Brumidi's work. *To Make Beautiful the Capitol: Rediscovering the Art of Constantino Brumidi* offers the perspectives of curators, historians, and fine art conservators stirred by Brumidi's newly revealed artistry. The conservation and study of the historic spaces that Brumidi decorated in the U.S. Capitol is complex, intriguing—and continuing.

Amy Elizabeth Burton
Office of Senate Curator

Opposite: Sketch showing a variety of brushes that Brumidi ordered for his work at the Capitol.

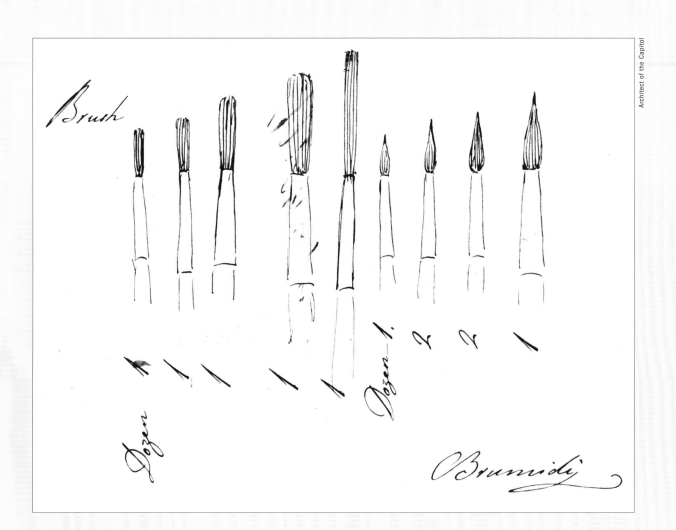

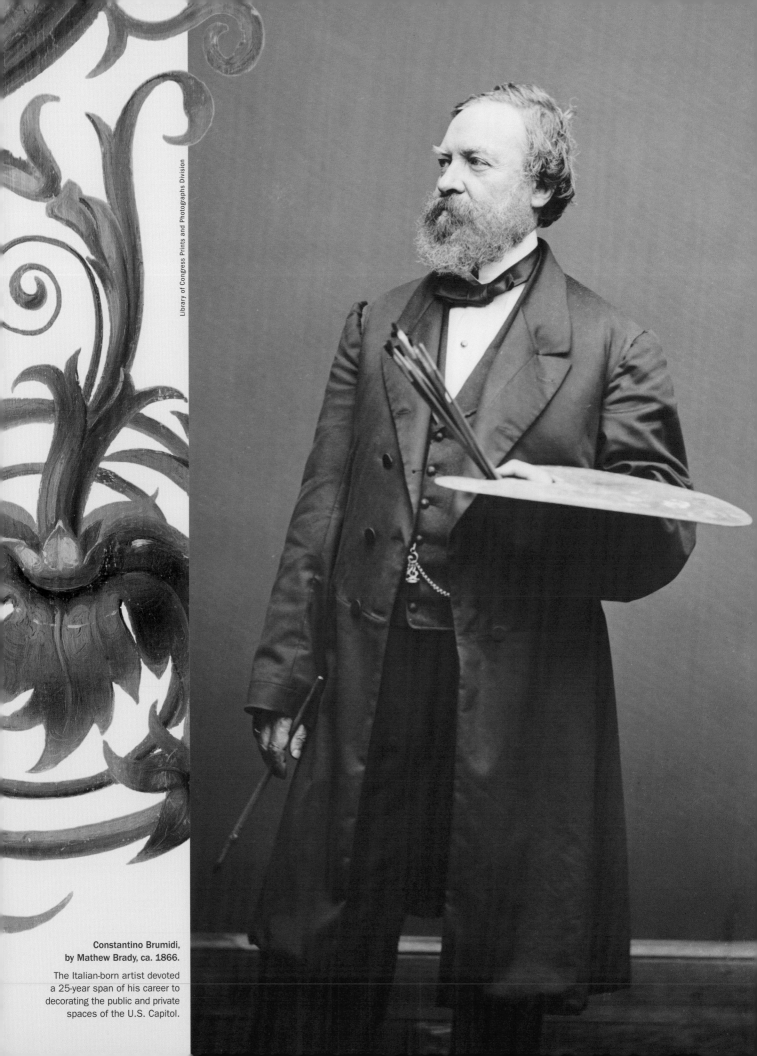

**Constantino Brumidi,
by Mathew Brady, ca. 1866.**

The Italian-born artist devoted
a 25-year span of his career to
decorating the public and private
spaces of the U.S. Capitol.

The Engineer and the Artist

MONTGOMERY C. MEIGS, CONSTANTINO BRUMIDI, AND THE CAPITOL FRESCOES

Donald A. Ritchie

Montgomery C. Meigs, the military engineer in charge of constructing the new Senate and House wings of the U.S. Capitol, photographed the fresco painter Constantino Brumidi in 1859. It had been four years since Meigs had hired Brumidi, whom Meigs described in his journal as an artist "full of genius and talent," able to design "with a fertility which is astonishing to me."[1] The engineer and the artist had collaborated to decorate the interiors of the expanded Capitol. Meigs' vision and Brumidi's skill endowed the building with its distinguished appearance, from the vivid colors and patterns selected for the tiled floors to the elaborate murals designed for the ceilings and walls. Meigs and Brumidi's partnership would soon end—for political reasons—but Brumidi would devote much of the next 20 years to the work he had begun under Meigs' supervision.

Far left: **Montgomery Cunningham Meigs, 1861.**

This photograph appears in the Brumidi family album.

Left: **Constantino Brumidi, 1859.**

Meigs' journal includes this photograph he took of the artist.

Opposite: **President's Room.**

The room illustrates Meigs' preference to give the Capitol extension elaborate interiors.

Their relationship is well documented, thanks to the journal that Meigs kept, although it was long inaccessible for scholarship because Meigs had recorded his thoughts in the Pitman style of shorthand. In the 1990s, the U.S. Senate Bicentennial Commission funded an extensive translation of the journal and employed the Senate's last reporter of debates to use Pitman shorthand, William D. Mohr. Published as *Capitol Builder: The Shorthand Journals of Montgomery C. Meigs, 1853–1859, 1861,* the journal records Meigs' multiple engineering duties and supervisory functions, as well as how he came to employ the talented Italian-born fresco and mural painter.

Born in 1816 in Augusta, Georgia, Montgomery Cunningham Meigs moved as a child with his family to Philadelphia. He was educated there at the school of the Franklin Institute and for a year at the University of Pennsylvania. At age 16, he entered the U.S. Military Academy at West Point, where he graduated fifth in his class in 1836 and then entered the Army Corps of Engineers. Meigs' mother recalled that, as a child, he was "high tempered, unyielding, tyrannical towards his brothers; very persevering in pursuit of anything he wishes."[2] Meigs later acknowledged that this portrait of the boy remained true of the man.

Meigs came to Washington, D.C., in 1852 to conduct a survey of how water from the Potomac River could be channeled via aqueducts from north of Great Falls into the city. He arrived in the midst of public controversy over the construction of the Capitol extension project. Crowded with additional members representing the new states entering the Union, Congress had authorized the enlargement of the Capitol, and President Millard Fillmore had appointed a professional architect, Thomas U. Walter of Philadelphia, to design the new wings. Accusations soon arose over the mishandling of contracts. Congress investigated and exonerated Walter, but the general superintendent of the project, Samuel Strong, resigned. Meanwhile, the Whig administration of Millard Fillmore was coming to an end, and a Democratic president, Franklin Pierce, would soon take office. Pierce concluded that a military engineer should be put in charge of the management of the Capitol extension. Consequently, in March of 1853, the construction project shifted to the War Department, headed by the new secretary of war, Jefferson Davis.

Secretary Davis had first put Captain Meigs in charge of building the Washington aqueduct and then saw him as the ideal person to supervise the Capitol construction. Combining technical skills with moral uprightness,

Meigs was also a Democrat in an army laden with Whig officers. With Davis' full support, Meigs simultaneously supervised the Washington aqueduct, the Capitol extension and new dome, the Post Office building expansion, and the construction of Fort Madison in Annapolis. "The management of all these works," he noted dryly, "give [sic] me ample employment."[3] These multiple projects required him to spend vast amounts of government money, and he was determined to do so honestly and without scandal. Once Meigs took charge of the Capitol extension, Thomas

Thomas Ustick Walter, by Francisco Pausas, oil on canvas, **1925**.

In 1851, President Fillmore approved Walter's plans for enlarging the Capitol and appointed him architect of the Capitol extension.

Walter was able to concentrate on architectural planning. But Walter would soon chafe at working under a strong-willed army officer. It particularly irked him that Meigs did not bother to consult with him when commissioning artwork and that Meigs sought only the approval of Secretary of War Davis.

Although Meigs admired Walter's plans for the exterior of the Capitol, he had other ideas for the building's interiors. Most dramatically, Meigs shifted the physical location of the House and Senate chambers away from the windows to the middle of the new wings. In designing the new wings, Walter had envisioned stone floors and plainly painted walls hung with an occasional painting. Meigs instead authorized colorful Minton tiles for the floors and had corridors and committee rooms decorated with murals. As a professional architect, Walter saw himself "contending for the dignity of our Profession against the assumptions and despotism of a military upstart who happens to have the power to annoy."[4] Walter urged his friends in Congress to keep

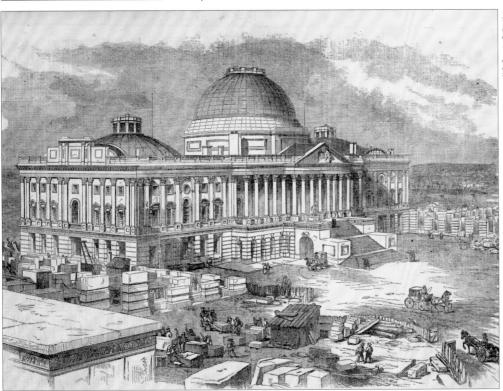

"Present State of the Capitol at Washington," *The Illustrated News*, engraving, January 8, 1853.

With construction of the Capitol extension well underway, Walter and Meigs clashed over designs for the interiors.

the Capitol extension "out of the hands of the military."[5] For his part, Meigs attributed their disputes to the nature of their "involuntary association."[6]

The army engineer surprised people with his "breadth of design, capacity of minute detail, and refined artistic taste."[7] Concerned with the appearance of space in the new wings as much as with its use, Meigs sought to educate himself about European wall decorations. He visited art galleries in New York and Philadelphia and consulted art books. He regretted that he had never visited Europe. "I ought to see the great buildings of the Old World before I finish the interior of the Capitol; for while I can form a good idea of the best examples of exterior architecture from drawings and engravings, we have nothing that gives a proper notion of the interior," he confided in his journal. "I fear that I may make the decoration tawdry instead of elegant, fall into a tavern instead of a palatial style."[8]

The existing Capitol did not lack decoration, including sculpture and the monumental Revolutionary War scenes painted by John Trumbull. The architecture and decorations of the early Capitol were in a neoclassical style, aiming for a republican form of art that would avoid the European vices of "over-refinement and luxury."[9] From his own studies in Philadelphia and at West Point, Meigs had come to admire Renaissance styles of architecture and decoration. In 1854, after looking at color plates in an art book of Raphael's loggia in the Vatican Palace, Meigs reflected: "I have never seen colored engraving of these works before. They are very beautiful, rich and harmonious in color, simple and beautiful in design. I wish I could see the rooms themselves."[10]

The engineer searched for artists with experience in wall and ceiling murals, but when he found that no American artists had experience with true fresco painting, he looked to European artists. This decision would put Meigs in conflict with the nativist, anti-immigrant, anti-Catholic, Know-Nothing ethos of the 1850s. Although Meigs wanted to promote American art, he was far less interested in nationality than in artistic skill.

At this juncture, Constantino Brumidi offered his services to decorate the Capitol's interiors. Born in Rome in 1805, Brumidi had studied at the Accademia di San Luca and helped restore frescoes at the Vatican. During the political turmoil of the Italian independence movement, Brumidi was arrested, imprisoned, and pardoned. He then thought it advisable to leave Italy. He arrived in New York in 1852. On December 28, 1854, he came to the Capitol accompanied by a Mr. Stone, likely the Washington physician-turned-sculptor, Horatio Stone, who introduced Brumidi to Meigs. In their first meeting, Meigs did not catch the artist's name, and so referred to him in his journal simply as a "lively old man" (although Brumidi was only a decade older than Meigs).[11] The artist had just returned from painting an altarpiece in the cathedral of Mexico City, and Meigs noted that Brumidi had "a very red nose, either from Mexican suns or French brandies."[12] Since Brumidi's English was rudimentary, the two men carried on their conversation in "bad French on both sides."[13] Brumidi spoke confidently of his skills and asked for a fresh wall where he could paint a sample of his work. Since Meigs' office was scheduled to become the House Agriculture Committee Room, Meigs identified a lunette over the entrance and asked Brumidi to plan an allegorical painting on agriculture. The artist said he had other work to do for a church and would be available to paint his sample in March, but Meigs explained that Brumidi's employment would depend on the members of Congress, who would be leaving the city right after the end of the session in March 1855. Quick to grasp political realities, Brumidi agreed that the church would always be there and that he should paint for the Congress first.

A month later, Brumidi presented an oil sketch of Cincinnatus at the plow—a popular theme of the citizen soldier called from agricultural pursuits to defend his nation. Meigs was taken with Brumidi's "skill in drawing and composition and coloring, much greater than I expected."[14] However, when Brumidi enlarged

his sketch to a full-sized drawing, the engineer was disappointed. "I did not think that he had carried out the promise of his sketch," he noted.[15] The figures now seemed carelessly drawn and out of proportion. Brumidi was not pleased to hear the critique, but Meigs warned him to expect such criticism. American painters were bound to be jealous of him and would "find all the fault they could" with his work.[16] The engineer worried about the artist's capabilities. "My Italian friend and fresco painter can no more paint an American than he could a Chinese scene," he ruminated. "He has no more idea of an Indian . . . than of the troops of the Emperor of Japan."[17]

Brumidi began making preparations for the fresco on February 14, 1855. The first step was "to wet thoroughly for several days the rough coat of plaster upon

Top: **Sketch for** *Calling of Cincinnatus from the Plow*, oil on canvas, 1855.

Bottom: **Calling of Cincinnatus from the Plow**, fresco, 1855.

Brumidi prepared a preliminary sketch of Cincinnatus at the plow for the room that was assigned to the House Agriculture Committee. After Meigs approved the sketch, Brumidi completed the scene in fresco.

the wall."[18] By February 19, the first section of plaster was ready, and Meigs watched with fascination as Brumidi mixed his palette, blending the colors with the lime on a slab of marble to create the tints he wanted. Brumidi reminded Meigs that the colors would change as they dried. At 10:30 that morning, the artist began painting. Meigs was surprised to see that Brumidi applied his colors in thick strokes and that the colors did not sink in as quickly as he expected. Meigs expressed his concern that the sky, laid on so thickly, would be too blue. Brumidi responded that he feared that it would prove too light. When Meigs left the office later that afternoon, Brumidi was still at work.

Day by day, the fresco progressed, fascinating the engineer. As Brumidi outlined the next figure, Meigs observed that the painting done the day before had come out with "more force and clearness" than at first.[19] Meigs was relieved to observe that, after three days, the original parts of the fresco showed "much improvement in clearness and beauty."[20] He also took note that the "mortar seems to set very hard, and it will make a durable wall, and the picture will be as durable as the wall itself."[21] Meigs invited visitors, especially members of Congress, to come and observe the artist at work. As the visitors streamed in, Brumidi ignored the crowds and continued painting rapidly. "The work thus far looks very strong and forcible," Meigs recorded with satisfaction.[22] He was still searching for American artists, but found that they charged "such high prices that I did not see how we could employ them."[23]

By March 15, 1855, Brumidi had completed *Calling of Cincinnatus from the Plow.* He then outlined his ideas for further projects, including a sketch (which he pronounced "skitch") of a painting of the four seasons for the Agriculture Committee room ceiling.[24] Meigs felt that it would "make a very beautiful room when finished" and was certain that "nothing so rich in effect" had ever been attempted on the American side of the Atlantic.[25] On the wall facing *Cincinnatus,* Brumidi would paint a companion fresco of General Israel Putnam being called from the plow during the American Revolution. To help the artist deal with American subjects, Meigs checked out from the Library of Congress a copy in Italian of Carlo Botta's *History of America.* Other scenes for the room included images of reaping by hand and by machine. Both the engineer and the artist shared a fascination with technology, and Meigs arranged for the manager of an agricultural warehouse to show Brumidi one of the latest McCormick reapers so that he could add it to the Agriculture Committee room's decorations.

Calling of Putnam from the Plow to the Revolution, fresco, 1855.

To help Brumidi create authentic American subjects for this mural, Meigs arranged for the Italian-born artist to study McCormick reapers and provided the artist with a book about the American Revolution.

Meigs hired Brumidi and a squad of other artists and artisans with plans to decorate another 80 rooms in the two wings. Meigs designated Brumidi as the "chief conductor" of the artistic projects, putting him on the payroll at a daily rate of $8, which was then equal to the pay of a member of Congress and the highest pay of any of the artists. Brumidi would do the true frescoes and would supervise the teams of painters handling other decorative elements. In dealing with these craftsmen, Brumidi showed himself to be above the petty jealousies that Meigs had encountered in so many "inferior artists."[26] Brumidi always seemed willing to praise good work by his assistants and went about his own work "with modesty and propriety" in the face of rising nativist criticism.[27] Brumidi's work gave Meigs a reference point for measuring the style of other artists and reinforced Meigs' confidence in his own artistic judgment. It also provided some pleasant diversions from the engineering challenges, financial headaches, and political interference Meigs encountered.

Meigs allowed an American artist, George R. West, to paint battle scenes in the Senate Naval Affairs Committee Room but disliked the result and had them removed. Once West's scenes were removed, Brumidi then executed the entire mural program. Between them, Meigs and Brumidi would give the

---

After that experience, Brumidi shied away from exclusively classical themes, incorporating more American imagery and historical scenes in his frescoes.

Capitol "a superior style of decoration in real fresco, like the palaces of Augustus and Nero . . . and the admired relics of the paintings at Herculaneum and Pompeii."[28] Adopting colors and motifs found in the murals at Pompeii, Brumidi painted images of Neptune and sea nymphs around the room's ceiling. Outraged critics called it "absurd" and "outrageous" to paint the room in a "servile, tasteless reproduction of the Pompeian style."[29] After that experience, Brumidi shied away from exclusively classical themes, incorporating more American imagery and historical scenes in his frescoes.

Not surprisingly, the Capitol construction attracted many job-seeking American artists, who expressed offense at finding Europeans decorating the halls of the U.S. Capitol. Nor were American artists modest about promoting their native-born skills. In February of 1857, an artist from St. Louis assured Meigs that Brumidi's fresco in the House Agriculture Committee Room was copied from a painting in Florence, and the artist insisted that he could paint something better. Meigs was unimpressed with both the man's drawings and his protestation that he usually designed as he painted. "This haphazard way of doing work may answer for the west," Meigs decided, "but in the Capitol I must know what is to be put upon a room before it begins."[30] Meigs rejected another artist's sketches for the Senate Library ceiling, regarding the figures as too large for the space, and selected Brumidi's plans instead. Meigs complained to Emmanuel Leutze, the German who was painting a large mural over the House stairs: "I have been annoyed by pretenders, by quacks, and by scholars. I have not received from any American artist a sketch or design for a picture fit to go into a county court house much less into the Capitol of the United States."[31]

Aware that critics regarded him as an engineer and "nothing more," Meigs had a strong desire to use his position "for the advancement of art in this country."[32] He was not "insensible to the honor of directing such a work as the Capitol," he told his father in March 1857. "My constructive facility is gratified in mastering its difficulties, in contriving the many machines and processes there used. My taste is gratified in the works of art, and my heart and conscience in the knowledge that, through me, much good flows

---

Opposite: **Senate Appropriations Committee Room.**

Brumidi's Pompeian decorative scheme for this room (originally the Naval Affairs Committee Room) sparked controversy.

to the laborer and to the artist and that to each and all is secured justice and courtesy." [33]

Trouble loomed when Franklin Pierce left office in 1857 and was replaced in the White House by the indecisive James Buchanan. In the new administration, the patronage-hungry John B. Floyd took over from Jefferson Davis as secretary of war. Davis assured Floyd of Meigs' many fine qualities: "When the work was transferred to the War Dept. I instituted careful inquiry to find a candidate competent by elementary preparation and practical application to carry on the magnificent project and who to these qualifications would add the moral attributes which would silence such complaints as had arisen both in regard to the purchase and the use of material. Good advice and

---

Davis wrote of Meigs: "Full of resources, above personal jealousy, calm, energetic, obliging, firm, discreet, just, patient to hear and willing to instruct, he soon overcame the prejudice against a military superintendent and acquired the confidence and the good will of the artists and workmen under his charge."

---

good fortune led me to select Capt. Meigs." [34] Davis wrote of Meigs: "Full of resources, above personal jealousy, calm, energetic, obliging, firm, discreet, just, patient to hear and willing to instruct, he soon overcame the prejudice against a military superintendent and acquired the confidence and the good will of the artists and workmen under his charge." [35]

Rejected artists and American nativists were raising a chorus of dissent over Brumidi's mythological images in the Capitol and attacked his style as "tawdry and gaudy ornaments, vile in taste, poor in design, and offensive in color" and "inappropriate to a Republic." [36] The American art establishment blamed Meigs for not hiring more native-born artists. "With

a fuller knowledge of the art-resources of the country," the editor of one art magazine sniffed, "more satisfactory results could have been effected with the same money." [37] One hundred and twenty-seven artists, among them such giants as Rembrandt Peale, Albert Bierstadt, and Thomas Sully, successfully petitioned Congress to create an art commission that would supplant Meigs' authority over art contracts. In May 1859, President Buchanan appointed three artists to the commission. One of the commissioners, Henry Kirke Brown, had submitted a proposal to do the pediment sculpture on the House side of the Capitol, which Meigs had rejected in part because it included a suffering slave sitting on a bale of cotton. Predictably, the art commission prepared a report that had little good to say of Brumidi's work, blasting the art of "an effete and decayed race which in no way represents us" and the "display of gaudy, inharmonious color" on the walls of the Capitol.[38] Whatever sympathy Congress might have felt for the report's call for more American art was counteracted by the commission's extravagant cost estimates for the work it envisioned. That spelled the end of the commission. Meigs commented acidly that the artists had only managed to endanger further congressional funding for art in the Capitol. Since he regarded the decorative mural painting as part of the building's construction, however, he was able to get the completion of the frescoes in the Senate wing included in the 1860 appropriations bill.

Congressional opinion divided over the Capitol's artwork. Some members of Congress admired the murals, while others were repelled by them. A mix of ideology and parochialism surfaced in the members' reactions. One western representative regretted that, in Brumidi's rendition of General Putnam at the plow, the artist had not shown a more modern western plow. Northern abolitionists thought there should have been some depiction of slave labor in the decorations. Meigs had advised artists to avoid controversial

Constantino Brumidi and his wife, Lola Germon Brumidi, as they appear in the Brumidi family album, ca. 1860–1880.

The Brumidi Family Photograph Album

Photographic albums enjoyed exceptional popularity in the Victorian era. They were used as memoirs and travelogues and often included images of prominent public figures. Commercially available albums held slots for cartes de visite, a popular and affordable form of photography often used as calling cards because of their small size. These albums became treasured family heirlooms, preserved as a collection and passed down from generation to generation. Mildred Thompson inherited such an album from her great grand-aunt, Lola Germon Brumidi, Brumidi's third wife. Thompson donated the album to the U.S. Senate in 1987.

Very little is known about Brumidi's personal life, and this photographic album provides insight into the artist and his family. The large, leather-bound book, with decorative pre-cut windows for cartes de visite, showcases 122 images of Brumidi, his family, and his friends, as well as paintings he completed outside the Capitol. The album contains images of public figures from Brumidi's time, such as President Lincoln, and it includes the likes of John Wilkes Booth, who performed on stage with Effie Germon, one of Brumidi's relatives. Her picture also appears in the album. Cartes de visite of Montgomery C. Meigs, Jefferson Davis, and Stephen Douglas, supporters of the artist and his efforts in decorating the Capitol, can be found next to more personal images of Brumidi's son Laurence, who matures from a child to a young man as the album pages progress.

themes, and instead of slavery, they had focused attention on Native Americans and western expansion. Brumidi's brightly painted ceiling beams in the new House of Representatives chamber struck some members as gaudy. A New York representative lamented that "Italian taste has exhibited on every side of this Hall the vermillion hue of Italy, instead of the sober, sensible hue of American intellect."[39] "Gaudy?" Meigs struck back. "But what is 'gaudy?' Are the colors of our autumnal forests gaudy?"[40]

Among his critics, Meigs faced renewed hostility from the Capitol architect. Taking advantage of the change in administration, Thomas U. Walter lobbied to remove the army engineer from his supervisory role at the Capitol. Walter admired Brumidi's artistry, but his strife with Meigs led him to publicly criticize the ornate decorations as "inappropriate" for rooms where committee business was supposed to occur. Some of these rooms were so extravagantly decorated, Walter complained, "that it is painful to remain in them."[41] Through all the flack, Brumidi kept working. Perhaps because he had been imprisoned in Italy for his political activities, he stayed out of the disputes swirling around his work in the Capitol. Brumidi became an American citizen in 1857. In a fresco depicting Cornwallis' surrender to Washington at Yorktown, painted in the House chamber, the artist added: "C. Brumidi Artist Citizen of the U.S."[42] This fresco remained in the House chamber until its 1950 remodeling and was later moved to the Members' Dining Room.

Suffering persistent interference from Secretary of War Floyd over contracts, Meigs protested to James Buchanan, but Meigs concluded that the secretary of war's "brute force of purpose and boldness" had overwhelmed the president's "timid caution and pusillanimity."[43] Buchanan could not settle the Meigs-Walter

Cornwallis Sues for Cessation of Hostilities under the Flag of Truce (detail), fresco, 1857.

Brumidi announced his new status as an American citizen with a signature and an inscription on the white strap.

dispute any more than he could hold the North and South together. In September 1860, Secretary Floyd removed Meigs from his Capitol job and dispatched him to the remote Tortugas to build forts off the Florida coast. Fortunately for Meigs, the Buchanan administration was ending, and in February 1861, he was ordered back to Washington, D.C. On March 4, Abraham Lincoln's inauguration took place in front of the unfinished Capitol dome. Meigs recorded in his diary that "we have at last found that we have a government." [44] President Lincoln was equally impressed with Meigs, whom he made quartermaster general of the Union Army in May of 1861. "I have come to know Colonel Meigs quite well for a short acquaintance," Lincoln wrote, "and so far as I am capable of judging, I do not know one who combines the qualities of masculine intellect, learning and experience of the right sort, and physical power of labor and endurance, so well as he." [45]

Although the war initially halted many Capitol projects, it did not interrupt construction of the new dome. In 1862, authority over the extension and dome was given to Walter, this time under the Interior Department rather than the War Department. With Meigs gone, Walter warmed to Brumidi's work and even hired the artist to paint rooms in his own house. In 1865, Walter commissioned Brumidi to paint the canopy of the Capitol's dome, having altered the architectural design to accommodate a monumental fresco. Brumidi would spend the rest of his career painting murals for the Capitol, many of them based on sketches that Meigs had approved before his banishment to the Tortugas.

General Meigs took pleasure in watching the artist's ongoing efforts. During the Civil War, Meigs assured the secretary of the interior that Brumidi's talents as a historical painter had "no equal in this country." [46] Meigs' only objection came when Brumidi painted Meigs into the scene of "Commerce" in *The Apotheosis*

Library of Congress Prints and Photographs Division

U.S. Senate Collection

Far left: **General Montgomery Cunningham Meigs, ca. 1865.**

Left: **"View of the Capitol, Showing Present State of the Dome.—Taken during the Inauguration of Lincoln, Monday, March 4, 1861,"** *Frank Leslie's Illustrated Newspaper,* engraving, March 16, 1861.

President Lincoln was inaugurated at the Capitol in March 1861. One month later, the Civil War began, and Lincoln appointed Meigs quartermaster general of the Union Army.

of *Washington* in the Rotunda. The engineer asked that his image be removed—fearing that it would open him to ridicule—and the artist complied. Viewing the finished *Apotheosis* in 1866, Meigs assured Brumidi that he found it "most agreeable and beautiful. The perspective is so well managed. . . . The figures appear to take

---

Meigs felt proud of his supervision of the Capitol extension and saw his patronage of the arts as his lasting legacy.

---

their places in space with the illusion of a diorama. I am glad the country at length possesses a Cupola on whose vault is painted a fresco picture after the manner of the great edifices of the old world."[47]

In defense of Brumidi's work, Meigs dismissed the critics of the Italian Renaissance style as those "who do not know that the finest models of architectural decoration, the works of Raphael and Da Vinci [sic], are copied and repeated upon the buildings of England and of this country."[48] In response to complaints about his insufficient nationalism, Meigs insisted that American artists lagged behind Europeans and failed to "surpass the highest efforts of older centuries."[49] Meigs felt proud of his supervision of the Capitol extension and saw his patronage of the arts as his lasting legacy. When he took charge of the Capitol project, Meigs pointed out, there had not been a single place designated for a statue. He had commissioned statues and sculptured bronze doors and had sponsored the frescoes for the Capitol's walls and ceilings. Writing to Brumidi on January 19, 1866, Meigs reflected on the works he had commissioned. "I have, I believe, been able to do much for American art."[50]

Right: **The Apotheosis of Washington** (detail), fresco, 1865.

Brumidi originally included Meigs' portrait in this scene of "Commerce," but at Meigs' insistence, Brumidi removed the likeness; the reworked area can still be discerned to the right of the money sack.

Opposite: **View of the Rotunda.**

Brumidi's monumental fresco, *The Apotheosis of Washington,* fills the Rotunda's canopy.

Architect of the Capitol

Blue-crowned Motmot,
Brumidi Corridors
(detail, North Corridor).

The Unlikely Significance of Brumidi's Motmot

Amy Elizabeth Burton

A groundbreaking discovery reveals the source of imagery for nearly four dozen birds painted in the Brumidi Corridors—the first such source to be identified for the corridors. This breakthrough deepens our understanding of the artist Constantino Brumidi and the way he worked when creating the murals in the Senate's renowned corridors. Moreover, the charming birds that enliven the walls of the Brumidi Corridors tell a fascinating and unexpected tale—a story that steps beyond ornithology and aesthetic appeal and points to a unique and important phase in America's growth as a nation and Congress' role in the physical and intellectual exploration of this vast new land.

For years, ornithologists speculated that Brumidi and his team of artists used some type of scientific reference for the paintings of birds in the Brumidi Corridors. The 345 birds are from such diverse geographic ranges that Brumidi could not have observed or sketched them from life, even if he had been an ornithological specialist. Although the birds are not depicted with scientific form or detail, they are represented with admirable verisimilitude. Brumidi clearly took great pains to include a substantial variety of birds from across North America in his designs for the murals, and many of the birds were recent ornithological observations from the American West. The newly discovered source for the birds sheds light on Brumidi's noteworthy accomplishment in rendering an estimated 200 species of birds in his murals.

The Tale of a Motmot

The discovery that finally linked Brumidi's birds to a specific source was many years in the making. It began as I watched the conservator of the Brumidi Corridors direct her work lamp on a mural of the distinctive motmot, a bird whose hallmark is its extraordinary tail feathers. Before restoration, the motmot was hardly inspiring. It bore a coat of clumsy overpaint and seemed dull, thickly executed, and unremarkable. As the conservator labored on this bird, she rescued its refinement and finesse. After restoration, Brumidi's motmot appeared resplendent. The recreation of feathers as rich and iridescent as a mallard's head—painted on plaster, no less—showcases the expertise, or *sprezzatura*, of a real master. The bird's stately elegance, as well as its very presence in the Brumidi Corridors, intrigued me. How did the Italian-born artist come to include this particular bird—remote and exotic by 1850s standards—here in the United States Senate?

After many years musing the riddle of this exceptional bird and its unlikely presence in the Capitol's murals, I was rewarded. As I thumbed through a 19th-century book in the Senate Library, the mirror-image of the motmot from the Brumidi Corridors stared out at me. It appeared that the motmot—as well as nearly four dozen

Right: **Motmot, Brumidi Corridors (North Corridor).**

Far right: **Mexican Boundary Report,** Plate VIII (*Momotus coeruleiceps*).

The motmot in the Brumidi Corridors bears a striking resemblance to that found in the *Mexican Boundary Report*.

"West End of Madelin Pass," *Pacific Railroad Report*, Volume 11, engraving, ca. 1861.

In the 19th century, federally sponsored expeditions included artists to document the flora and fauna of the land.

of Brumidi's other birds—derived from two weighty congressional publications printed from 1855 to 1861: *Report on the United States and Mexican Boundary Survey* and *Reports of Explorations and Surveys, to Ascertain the Most Practicable and Economical Route for a Railroad from the Mississippi River to the Pacific Ocean.*

The *Mexican Boundary Report* and the *Pacific Railroad Report* provided comprehensive descriptions of the nation's newly surveyed geographical regions and included beautifully illustrated sections dedicated to ornithology. The birds identified on the expeditions and illustrated in the reports evidently provided a rich and inspiring source of subject matter for the decorative wall paintings in the Capitol. However, Brumidi's use of the reports as reference material was not a documented part of the Capitol's history, and the reports' influence on Brumidi's murals had long since faded from institutional memory.

Fortunately, copies of the *Mexican Boundary Report* and the *Pacific Railroad Report* never strayed far from the Capitol. As Brumidi and his assistants painted the corridors in the 1850s, the reports were delivered directly to the Capitol, specifically for Congress' use. The Senate's chief clerk collected reports to Congress prior to the 1871 founding of the Senate Library, and later, the Senate Library would count the volumes in its holdings.

For nearly 150 years, these books and their ornithological lithographs have been waiting to be rediscovered and reassociated with Brumidi's work in the Capitol.

A Triad: Congress, Exploring Expeditions, and the Smithsonian Institution

The connection between Brumidi's murals and the *Mexican Boundary* and *Pacific Railroad* reports now lends an historical relevance to the birds of the Brumidi Corridors. Placed in context, Brumidi's birds reflect the 19th-century surge in westward expansion and federal support for exploration and scientific discovery across the young and developing nation.

The 1830s through the 1880s witnessed America's great age of transcontinental exploration. Prompted by growing economic and strategic interests, federally sponsored expeditions mapped boundaries, ascertained rail routes, and explored the geological history and diverse resources of the trans-Mississippi West. Congress appropriated funds for these important expeditions and the resulting public reports. This investment promoted "nation-building," fitting for the Manifest Destiny generations of the mid-19th century. It also cultivated national scientific advancement and allowed a young America to plant its flag in the scientific world.

In 1846, Congress enacted legislation to establish the Smithsonian Institution "for the increase and diffusion of knowledge among men."[1] Regarded as the national museum, the Smithsonian Institution supplied federally funded expeditions with naturalists and collectors and became the repository for all federal science collections. As a result of the numerous and extensive expeditions, the fledgling museum experienced explosive growth as a collecting institution. The Smithsonian Institution also assumed responsibility for the wide-ranging scientific content published in the congressional reports from the government-sponsored expeditions. To appreciate the full story that the Capitol's birds tell, one must first study the ambitious *Mexican Boundary* and *Pacific Railroad* reports and the man instrumental to their creation, Spencer Fullerton Baird.

Spencer Baird (1823–1887) was the quiet but indefatigable force behind 26 government-sponsored exploring expeditions in the mid-19th century. As a well-educated and driven youth, he focused on ornithology. At age 17, Baird wrote to John James Audubon, the legendary ornithologist. Baird hoped that he had discovered a new type of bird but admitted that his descriptions might seem "very inexperienced" to this paragon of the field. Audubon confirmed the new species and added amiably, "although you speak of yourself as being a youth, your style and the descriptions you have sent me prove to me that an old head may from time to time be found on young shoulders."[2] Baird and Audubon continued their friendship until Audubon's death in 1851.

Baird's career would eventually take him far beyond the specialized field of ornithology. In 1850, at age 27, he became assistant secretary of the Smithsonian Institution. Baird's industriousness at the Smithsonian was legendary. During his career, he catalogued the findings from 1,000 of his carefully selected field collectors. As assistant secretary, and later as secretary of the Smithsonian, Baird played a critical role in the scientific exploration of the American West. He organized provisions and trained naturalists for the government's exploring expeditions. With his guidance

U.S. Senate Collection

"Balloon View of Washington, D.C." (detail), *Harper's Weekly*, engraving, July 27, 1861.

The Smithsonian Institution's first building was constructed in 1855, as seen in the background of this engraving.

National Museum of American History, Smithsonian Institution

Spencer Fullerton Baird, daguerreotype, 1842.

As a young man, Baird began a correspondence with prominent ornithologist John James Audubon.

and expertise, the resulting collections came to the Smithsonian Institution as part of a national collecting plan. Baird worked with exquisite timing, right as the government's systematic exploration of the trans-Mississippi West surged, in the era dubbed the "Great Reconnaissance." With his well-chosen connections in numerous branches of government, and with a father-in-law serving as inspector general of the United States Army and in charge of all terrestrial exploration, Baird earned a reputation as a "collector of collectors" and counted among his agents such luminaries as Commodore Matthew Perry, Captain David Farragut, and General George McClellan.[3]

A Grand Compendium

As if these credentials were not enough, Baird also acted as supervisor of publications at the Smithsonian Institution and shaped the appearance, content, and quality of expedition reports. He prepared the ornithological descriptions and drew the 25 ornithological illustrations found in the *Mexican Boundary Report*. Issued in two volumes from 1857 to 1859, this impressive publication documented and mapped the nearly 2,000-mile boundary between the United States and Mexico following the Mexican-American War in 1846–48. Thanks to Baird's influence, the authoritative work served as a "grand compendium," rich with descriptions and illustrations of the flora, fauna, geography, and natural history of the region. At the time, renowned Harvard botanist Asa Grey proclaimed, "It must be ranked as the most important publication of the kind that has ever appeared."[4]

Right, top: **Mexican Boundary Report, Plate XVIII** (*Cyanoloxia parellina* and *Spiza versicolor*).

Right, center and bottom: **Indigo Bunting and Varied Bunting, Brumidi Corridors (North Corridor).**

Evidence suggests that ornithological prints served as inspiration for Brumidi's murals in the Senate's corridors. Here, the birds' poses were altered to create a sense of spontaneity and flight.

A Railroad to the Pacific Ocean

Baird also authored and reviewed several of the 12 encyclopedic volumes of the *Pacific Railroad Report*.[5] In 1853, Congress appropriated $340,000 for multiple expedition parties to survey potential routes across the West for the first transcontinental railroad. The Pacific railroad expeditions of 1853–54 collected a cornucopia of information about the natural history of the region. Topographical engineers, cartographers, physicians, naturalists, geologists, meteorologists, and botanists joined the parties of military engineers assigned to gather information. All of the ornithological descriptions and illustrations from the *Pacific Railroad Report* were ultimately reviewed by Baird and published to his exacting standards.

"Induce Them to Continue Such Explorations"

Baird worked tirelessly during his career at the Smithsonian Institution to publish high-quality reports for 26 federally sponsored expeditions. He felt a keen responsibility to curate a public collection and produce publications that would encourage the respect of the scientific world. Baird's insistence on quality elevated the artistic integrity of these congressional publications. Baird was savvy and recognized that high-caliber publications were instrumental in convincing Congress of the merit of appropriating funds for the expeditions and the subsequent reports.

When Baird assumed his role at the Smithsonian in 1850, he inherited a problem: Congress was still smarting from the poorly administered U.S. Exploring Expedition of 1838–42, which had cost a whopping $928,000. As late as 1861, Senator Simon Cameron of Pennsylvania declared, "I am tired of all this thing called science here. It was only the other day we made another appropriation in regard to the expedition which Captain Wilkes took out to the Pacific ocean. We have paid $1,000 a volume for the book which he published. Who has ever seen that book outside of this Senate, and how many copies are there of it in this country?"[6]

Baird's integrity, vision, and successful management of the exploring expeditions and publication program helped regain Congress' support. Writing to one of his lithographers, Baird urged, "I trust these plates of yours to make such an impression on Congress as will induce them to continue such explorations; and publish the results in creditable style."[7] Baird ensured that the lithographs for the *Mexican Boundary Report* were prepared by none other than J.T. Bowen and Company—the same establishment that had prepared Audubon's lavish octavo edition of *Birds of America*. For the *Pacific Railroad Report*, Baird invested in the services of the reputable John Cassin, curator of the Philadelphia Academy of Natural Sciences. Baird paid Cassin $5,324 to draw, print, and hand color 2,000 copies each of 38 plates of birds. These illustrations are a credit to Spencer Baird's vision and merit a place among distinguished American ornithological works.

The art of ornithological illustration reached its height in the 19th century with hand-colored lithography, the medium of choice for the 58 ornithological illustrations published in the *Mexican Boundary* and *Pacific Railroad* reports. These exceptional plates testify to Baird's commitment to the advancement of American science. Hand coloring was laborious and costly but produced prints seldom surpassed in beauty or color accuracy by other printing methods in pre-Civil War America. For the two reports' ornithology sections alone, more than 100,000 lithographs were meticulously colored by hand.

Renaissance of the Brumidi Birds

Without extensive restoration of the Brumidi Corridors, the connection between the Senate's birds and the *Mexican Boundary* and *Pacific Railroad* reports might never have been made. Once muddied by amateurish retouching, the birds of the Brumidi Corridors have enjoyed a renaissance following restoration that unveils their original plumage and splendor. Having molted dull, awkward layers of overpaint and varnish, the birds can be identified by species and studied in earnest.

Restoration in progress, Woodhouse's Jay, Brumidi Corridors (North Entry).

Inexpert overpaint made the bird indistinguishable as a species. Notice how the wing shape and plumage color changed as layers of overpaint accumulated. The restored bird regained its delicate grace.

Restoring the Senate's Birds

Constantino Brumidi and his assistant artists executed the majority of the Brumidi Corridors between 1857 and 1859.

As decades passed, the condition of the corridors deteriorated. Nineteenth-century methods of heating and lighting the Capitol created smoke and soot, which darkened the surface of Brumidi's murals. Aged varnish, which yellows and attracts a dulling film of dust, also marred the once-fresh look of the corridors. Subsequent generations repainted the murals using incorrect colors, replicating and perpetuating the aged and dingy appearance. Inexpert retouching compounded the problems by distorting the refinement of the original shapes and details in the paintings.

By the time conservators embarked on a major restoration campaign in 1996, the Brumidi Corridors suffered from multiple layers of overpaint applied in the intervening century. Conservators carefully removed these layers in a restoration effort directed by the Architect of the Capitol's curator. Today, the Brumidi Corridors appear with their original splendor, detail, and vibrancy.

Top: **Mexican Boundary Report**, Plate XIX (*Icterus parisorum* and *Icterus wagleri*).

Bottom: **Black-vented Oriole, Brumidi Corridors (North Entry).**

Accurate eye and leg colors suggest that the artist relied on illustrations, not just specimen skins, when replicating birds in the Brumidi Corridors' murals.

Until the discovery of the *Mexican Boundary* and *Pacific Railroad* reports, little was known about Brumidi's sources or methods for selecting and replicating the flora and fauna of the Brumidi Corridors. A solitary clue originated in an 1874 guide book, *Keim's Illustrated Hand-Book*. It states that the birds in the Capitol "are studies from the collection in the Museum in the Smithsonian Institution, drawn by Brumidi."[8] For many years, it was assumed that "studies" referred to the Smithsonian's extensive collection of specimen skins. However, experts found this assumption problematic. Because soft tissues deteriorate and seldom reflect the true nature of the living bird, skins would not have provided reliable data for eye or leg colors. After restoration of the Brumidi Corridors, accurate details in

---

Until the discovery of the Mexican Boundary *and* Pacific Railroad *reports, little was known about Brumidi's sources or methods for selecting and replicating the flora and fauna of the Brumidi Corridors.*

Brumidi's birds became discernible and suggested that the artist looked to precise scientific illustrations, not just specimen skins. The hint provided in *Keim's* perhaps pointed all these years to Baird's lithographs.

From Baird's Lithographs to Brumidi's Murals

The ornithological sections of the *Mexican Boundary* and *Pacific Railroad* reports were published by the government between 1857 and 1860 and would have rolled hot off the press in precisely the years that Brumidi and his team of artists decorated the Brumidi Corridors.

Although Brumidi was the chief artist responsible for the overall design of the murals, his was not the only hand to paint the corridors. The English painter James Leslie was believed to be Brumidi's best assistant at depicting birds and animals, but Brumidi oversaw several artists, many of Italian and German descent, who specialized in painting flowers, fruits, faux moldings, landscapes, and animals.

Brumidi and his team of artists created a unified overall effect in the elaborate Brumidi Corridors, but a close analysis of the murals reveals subtle stylistic differences in the execution of the birds. Some poses are full of motion and give a feeling of the living bird, indicating an artist confident enough to take license with the specimens in the pages of the source books. Other birds in the murals replicate the more static poses of the birds in the reports, perhaps done by a different painter in Brumidi's crew. At times, the artists even copied the specific leaves and branches found in the lithographs.

Right: **Mexican Boundary Report**, Plate III (*Picus scalaris* and *Picus nuttallii*).

Below: **Ladder-backed Woodpecker, Brumidi Corridors (North Entry).**

Several birds in the Brumidi Corridors are literal translations from the expedition reports. Here, the mirror-image pose of the woodpecker, as well as the shape of the leaves, is taken directly from the lithograph.

Interestingly, the birds modeled after the illustrations in the *Mexican Boundary* and *Pacific Railroad* reports appear in three specific areas of the Brumidi Corridors. This placement suggests that Brumidi and his assistants used the reports as they systematically executed portions of the wall murals in the expansive network of corridors.

The Brumidi Corridors' largest hallway, the North Corridor, showcases specimens from the reports in seven out of eight of its most prominent panels. Brumidi often adapted the lithographed bird's pose, or reversed it, to avoid repetition in the murals. On occasion, the reports' specimens appear almost traced onto the murals. Artistic license was duly exercised in just as many instances, with some of the birds enlarged or

Left: Mexican Boundary Report, Plate XXII *(Cyanocitta sordida).*

The reports' lithographs typically illustrate one specimen per species.

Below: Mexican Jay, Brumidi Corridors (North Corridor).

In the North Corridor, Brumidi adapted the lithographs to create formal-looking pairs of birds flanking vessels abundant with fruits and flowers.

Pacific Railroad Report, Plate XXXVI (*Centurus uropygialis*).

The Gila Woodpecker was first identified in 1854 during expeditions that surveyed potential routes for the first transcontinental railroad.

Gila Woodpecker, Brumidi Corridors (North Entry).

Brumidi included the newly discovered woodpecker in his murals shortly after the species was illustrated in the *Pacific Railroad Report*.

reduced in size. Priority seems to have been placed on the aesthetics of the murals as a whole rather than on the accurate representation to scale of the various species.

Individual specimens from the *Mexican Boundary* and *Pacific Railroad* reports cluster in the North Corridor's perpendicular spurs. One of these two spurs is the North Entry, a handsome foyer where nearly all of the 17 birds match those in the *Mexican Boundary* and *Pacific Railroad* reports. Unfortunately, two of the birds in these murals were badly damaged and could not be restored to Brumidi's original, so we will never know their true appearance or source. The Zodiac Corridor, the second spur that runs parallel to the North Entry, contains 22 birds, half of which were drawn from the reports.

In total, Brumidi adapted over 30 species of birds from the *Mexican Boundary Report* and *Pacific Railroad Report* for use in the Senate's murals. He used

several species more than once, so that 46 birds in the Brumidi Corridors appear as if issued from the pages of the congressional reports.

Brumidi's murals are a time capsule of sorts. Mixed within the medley of birds common to the eastern states are leading-edge ornithological discoveries from territories in the West still being explored and settled. The Gila Woodpecker, for instance, makes an appearance in Brumidi's murals. This species was first identified in 1854 on the Pacific railroad expeditions and was illustrated in 1859 in volume 10 of the *Pacific Railroad Report*. Most Americans would not have seen this bird firsthand or in prior publications. Its presence in Brumidi's murals speaks volumes about the impact of 19th-century science and exploration on the psyche of the nation. Even the gentle birds of Brumidi's murals captured and celebrated the expanding bounty and variety that America had to offer.

Meigs, Sources, and Brumidi

The many birds ornamenting the Brumidi Corridors' murals are part of a long artistic tradition. Birds depicted with charming naturalism enliven ancient Roman mosaics and wall paintings. More directly, the mural designs of the loggia in the Vatican Palace influenced the delicate birds in the Senate's corridors. The murals in Raphael's early 16th-century loggia include a variety of birds nestled within a sophisticated framework of classical ornamentation. Today, the condition of the murals in the loggia is compromised, and a great many of the details are lost, but in the 1840s, Brumidi had worked at the Vatican and was familiar with its legendary designs.

Trained in Italy, Brumidi was well versed in the classical tradition and brought its distinct look to the Capitol. Montgomery C. Meigs, supervising engineer of the Capitol extension, desired that the Capitol's interiors rival those of Europe's great edifices and specified in his journal that Raphael's work at the Vatican would "give us ideas in decorating our lobbies."[9] Within Brumidi's first few years at the Capitol, he skillfully adapted many classical decorative arrangements for the Brumidi Corridors and added a bounty of motifs that reflected American interests. Perched in the ancient Roman arabesques and vines are sensitively rendered North American birds. Although one section of the Brumidi Corridors contains a handful of birds from foreign lands, such as parrots from Latin America and a Eurasian Hoopoe, the majority of birds are native species.

To render the impressive variety of specimens in his murals that perch, peck, and take wing throughout the stately corridors, Brumidi evidently utilized reference materials, such as the *Mexican Boundary* and *Pacific Railroad* reports. Using reference materials was not an uncommon practice for him. In 1858, a newspaper correspondent reported that Brumidi's work at the Capitol was done "with the aid of native pictures and engravings."[10] Meigs

Panel with birds, Brumidi Corridors (West Corridor).

Brumidi placed North American birds within the classical scrolling vines.

Exotic parrots, Brumidi Corridors (North Corridor).

Only a small number of specimens in the Brumidi Corridors are non-native species, such as the parrots seen above.

*Above left: **National Museum Building Committee**, 1880.*

Shown here during their collaboration on construction of the Smithsonian Institution Arts and Industries Building, Meigs, *far left*, and Baird, *fourth from right*, were colleagues throughout their careers in Washington, D.C.

occasionally provided Brumidi with books and prints to help the Italian-born artist develop accurate historical scenes and to depict authentic details. An album filled with clippings of architectural engravings that belonged to Brumidi indicates that he, too, kept material for artistic inspiration. The margins are inked with Brumidi's sketches and doodles. As an academy-trained artist, Brumidi would have been accustomed to using many types of reference materials to create detailed and complex paintings.

The *Mexican Boundary* and *Pacific Railroad* reports documented species abundant during the 1850s exploration of the trans-Mississippi West. Brumidi featured these ornithological specimens in his murals when he was in his early 50s. When Brumidi passed away at age 75 in 1880, Senator Daniel Vorhees of Indiana noted the vast changes to the American landscape during his eulogy to the late artist:

> To one who recalls the great forests of the West before they were swept away, the birds and the specimens of American animals with which [Brumidi] has adorned a portion of this Capitol must be a source of unceasing enjoyment. The birds especially are all there, from the humming-bird at an open flower to the bald eagle with his fiery eye and angry feathers. I have been told that the aged artist loved these birds as a father loves his children and that he often lingered in their midst as if a strong tie bound him to them.[11]

The Final Mystery

How exactly the *Mexican Boundary* and *Pacific Railroad* publications came into Brumidi's hands may never be known. Meigs and Baird were colleagues and communicated throughout their careers in Washington, D.C. However, there is no specific record mentioning the Brumidi Corridors' birds in Meigs' own journal. Furthermore, a fire in 1865 destroyed the Smithsonian Institution's early records and would have destroyed any mention of this topic that Baird may have recorded.

Did Meigs, or perhaps Brumidi, discover the handsome *Mexican Boundary* and *Pacific Railroad* reports when they were delivered to Congress? Could Baird, wishing to foster the Smithsonian's relationship with Congress, have suggested the illustrations to Meigs for the Capitol's decorative scheme? No matter the "how," these publications' influence on the Brumidi Corridors is evident and undeniable, and most importantly, has contributed to a fuller understanding of the history of the Capitol and the men who shaped it.

Restoration has changed what we know about the artist Constantino Brumidi, his methods, and the Senate's historic and meaning-filled decorative program. No detail is too small to be denied a significance or purpose. To date, only four dozen of the 345 birds in the Brumidi Corridors have an identified source—which means additional discovery lies ahead for those who are willing to let curiosity lead them forward.

Cabbage White butterfly, Brumidi Corridors (West Corridor).

Brumidi's Cabbage White Butterfly (*Pieris rapae*)

Generations of children have grown up chasing the ubiquitous Cabbage White butterfly in backyards across America. This butterfly, now commonplace throughout the nation, is not native to the United States and is a relatively recent arrival. At the time Constantino Brumidi painted the Senate's corridors in the late 1850s, the Cabbage White butterfly had yet to spread across North America. How, then, did Brumidi come to paint this insect in the Capitol?

Interestingly, all of the 13 identifiable butterfly species in the Brumidi Corridors are European, including the Cabbage White (*Pieris rapae*). Brumidi was known to utilize reference books for his mural work; however, American butterfly identification guides were not common in his time. European reference books were more widely published then, which may explain why European butterflies predominate in the Senate's corridors.

The acclaimed 19th-century lepidopterist Samuel Scudder traced the spread of *Pieris rapae* and concluded that the species arrived on cabbages accompanying European immigrants. Introduced to North America via Quebec in the 1850s, the species reached New England by 1871. Within a quarter century after its arrival in the U.S., widespread colonization of the Cabbage White butterfly resulted in significant crop losses to the cabbage family, and this insect gained notoriety as one of the earliest observed, non-native species to affect North American agriculture.

Today, this butterfly's range reaches across the entire nation, but at the time Brumidi painted the corridors that bear his name, this pearly white "crop pest" was just a distant specimen in a book of butterfly illustrations.

Peace and Architecture, Brumidi Corridors (West Corridor).

A section of overpaint remains on the face of Peace, *left*, and shows alterations made to Brumidi's murals in the 19th and early 20th centuries.

Uncovering the Historic Roots of Brumidi's Decorations

AN INTERVIEW WITH CONSERVATOR CHRISTIANA CUNNINGHAM-ADAMS

With deft turns of a steel surgical scalpel, fine art conservator Christiana Cunningham-Adams removed thick layers of disfiguring overpaint from the wall murals in the Brumidi Corridors and discovered the exquisite artistry of Constantino Brumidi hidden underneath. Her initial test of the murals, followed by a one-year technical study in 1993, developed into a major conservation project to restore the Brumidi Corridors to their original appearance. The murals had been sorely compromised by more than a century of age, damage, and alterations by later artists in the form of heavy overpaint. Through Cunningham-Adams' perseverance and skilled hand, the integrity of the mural designs has reemerged and has paved the way to a renewed appreciation of the technical and historical character of Brumidi's painting. In an interview with the Office of Senate Curator, Cunningham-Adams shares her professional experience and unique insights as principal conservator of the Brumidi Corridors restoration effort.[1]

Office of Senate Curator: Restoring the Brumidi Corridors to their original appearance is a monumental task that has already taken nearly two decades and is slated to take five more years to finish. Why has it been important to undertake this project at the Capitol?

Cunningham-Adams: The project is important for many reasons. The original artwork that we have been uncovering reveals highly refined artistic effects that have been hidden for more than a century. By recovering the aesthetic sophistication of Brumidi's original artwork, the restoration also reveals what I believe was the original intent—for the decoration to connect our new democracy with some of history's highest cultural achievements. In creating his ornamental program for the walls and ceilings of the Capitol, Brumidi referenced a decorative tradition fashioned more than 2,000 years ago by the ancient Romans. Revived and modified by artists in the Italian Renaissance of the 15th and 16th centuries, and again in the neoclassical era of the 18th and early 19th centuries, the historic decorative style was further tailored to America with Brumidi's own inspired interpretation. The connections to antiquity are more vividly apparent now that conservation has removed the layers of overpaint that obscured Brumidi's murals and his artistic vision for these public spaces. The original beauty and sophistication of the decoration is thus being recovered with the restoration project, and conservation is giving back the Capitol interiors their true quality and context.

What was Constantino Brumidi's background, and how did he come to undertake the challenge of decorating the Capitol interiors?

Born in Rome in 1805, Brumidi showed artistic talent as a child. At the age of 13, he entered Rome's prestigious art school, the Accademia di San Luca, where he studied for 14 years. He developed technical proficiency in classical painting and sculpture and was

George W. Adams

Putti, Brumidi Corridors (North Corridor).
Brumidi's style is evident in even the minutest details of his murals, such as the diminutive putti with their graceful stance and the scrolling vines that delicately frame the figures.

awarded prizes for his outstanding abilities. Brumidi enjoyed a successful career as an artist and decorative painter in Italy. However, in 1851, he was arrested for what was regarded as revolutionary activity during a period of political upheaval in Rome. The pope pardoned Brumidi and allowed him to immigrate to the United States in 1852. Arriving in New York City, Brumidi started a new chapter in his life. He learned of the need to decorate the Capitol extension, which was then under construction, and came to Washington, D.C., in 1854 to inquire about employment. Montgomery C. Meigs, supervising engineer of the Capitol extension, had a preference for decorating the House and Senate wings with the "European style," so when Brumidi presented his credentials to Meigs, he was the right person in the right place at the right time.

Left: **Ceiling mural, Brumidi Corridors (Zodiac Corridor).**

Above left: **Ceiling mural, Palazzo Vecchio, Florence, Italy, 16th century.**

Above center: **Wall mural, Villa Poppaea, Oplontis, Italy, 1st century B.C.**

Above right: **Wall mural, Brumidi Corridors (West Corridor).**

Brumidi's wall and ceiling murals in the U.S. Capitol reference the motifs and designs typical of ancient Roman and Renaissance decorative work.

What was it that made Brumidi the right person to decorate the Capitol's interiors?

When Brumidi immigrated to the United States at 47 years of age, he was a mature artist with a wealth of experience and technical skill. Brumidi had designed and executed large-scale decorative programs for some of Rome's expansive neoclassical villas and palaces and had also worked at the Vatican Palace in the 1840s for Pope Gregory XVI. Brumidi's expertise struck a chord with Meigs, who envisioned classical-style designs for the artwork in the Capitol's interiors. Brumidi was the right person for the job of ornamenting the rooms and corridors in the U.S. Capitol because he was thoroughly familiar with classical and Renaissance motifs, patterns, and techniques.

Why was extensive conservation necessary in the Brumidi Corridors?

As Brumidi's wall and ceiling murals darkened and dirtied due to age and environmental damage, they were periodically "refurbished" during the 19th and 20th centuries. However, instead of cleaning the murals, the painters who did the touch-ups simply repainted the historic murals by matching the increasingly dirty and discolored surfaces. This practice eventually buried Brumidi's work under layers of added paint that reflected little of the original quality. Brumidi's painting has a lyrical beauty and technical competence that compares with ancient Roman and Renaissance decorative work of the same genre, and conservation of the murals has helped uncover the exceptional skill of Brumidi and his team of artists.

Restored wall murals in 2004, Brumidi Corridors (North Corridor).

The extensive wall mural conservation project involved plaster consolidation, overpaint removal, stabilization and infilling of losses in the original paint layer, and finally, varnishing of the corridors' 153 panels.

How do you and your team of conservators restore Brumidi's murals?

The restoration methods depend on the medium as well as the condition of the murals. Brumidi employed a range of paint media in his work at the Capitol, from delicate water-based tempera to more durable oil emulsion tempera and fresco. We spent well over a decade to work our way systematically through the elaborate wall murals in the Patent, North, and West Corridors (including the North Entry), and then the Zodiac Corridor. In the long North Corridor, for example, it appeared that Brumidi had used a type of lime wash fresco, in which many of the murals' details were painted onto a wet layer of calcium hydroxide, or slaked lime. Some of the details painted onto the white lime background were then rendered brighter with colors added in tempera. In other corridors,

it appeared that the wall murals were painted in oil emulsion tempera. The strong and flat surfaces that Brumidi produced with these types of paint media allowed our conservation team to use surgical scalpels to carefully slice away the added layers of overpaint. We found that the masterful brushwork, limpid colors, and exquisite detail in Brumidi's decorations were often hidden by six or more layers of overpaint, and that in many cases, the original surfaces were largely intact and recoverable.

The process of conserving these types of murals demands that a conservator focus on a surface area of only two to three inches at a time, which requires strict concentration, patience, and precision. We cannot remove the overpaint with solvents because the layers of overpaint are too thick or we might stain the original surface by putting the overpaint into solution.

When we find deteriorated areas in the original surface, such as flaking paint or old scratches and gouges, we stabilize these damaged areas, fill the depressions with a fine putty of gesso, and then retouch the puttied fills with watercolors. We prefer to use watercolors because they are chemically stable and easily reversible, if necessary. Also, the delicate transparency of watercolors best simulates aged paint that becomes somewhat transparent over time. We do not repaint the original surface in cases like this, but instead merely repair areas where paint is missing. Finally, we apply a matte varnish that seals the retouching and provides protection from the environment and from the damaging effects of human hands that might touch the walls.

Right: **Charles Whipple repainting the Brumidi Corridors, ca. 1920.**

Below: **Conservation test exposure showing overpaint layers and original mural designs, Brumidi Corridors (North Entry).**

Overpaint altered the appearance of the murals in the Brumidi Corridors. Numbered arrows indicate the six layers of overpaint applied successively over a century to the original surface.

Unlike the walls, the ceilings in the Brumidi Corridors were painted in tempera, a very delicate, porous medium. Where oil-based overpaint was applied to the ceiling murals, it penetrated the tempera, sometimes producing an irreversible bond. In some of these areas, we have had to replicate the original effects on top of the later overpaint, in order to recover the aesthetic character of the 19th-century decoration.

Before addressing the paint layers in the murals, however, we first examine and treat instabilities that we detect in the underlying plaster. We evaluate and document the different types of plaster failures, including the breakdown of the plaster itself or its failure to adhere to the architectural substrate. We then fortify any deficient areas to restore the integrity of the walls or ceilings supporting the paintings.

Our conservation team's engineer, George W. Adams, developed a consolidation technique tailored to the particular plaster deficiencies found in the Brumidi Corridors. The system—essentially a reservoir of consolidant connected to the substrate by a tube—allows infusion of the consolidant into the plaster at a controlled and slow rate of pressure. This delivery system enables the plaster to more thoroughly accept the consolidant. As the mural's support, the plaster and its condition are essential in securing the continued preservation of the painting.

George W. Adams

Architect of the Capitol

Above left: **Plaster instabilities identified in *The Signing of the First Treaty of Peace with Great Britain*, fresco, 1874, Brumidi Corridors (North Corridor).**

The condition of the underlying plaster is determined so that any deficiencies can be stabilized. Indicated in red are areas where the plaster detached from the architectural substructure, requiring consolidation. Indicated in blue are areas to monitor.

Left: **Christy Cunningham-Adams addressing overpaint removal on a tempera ceiling mural, Brumidi Corridors (Zodiac Corridor).**

Cunningham-Adams has devoted the greater part of two decades to restoring Brumidi's murals in the Capitol.

Fruit cluster before conservation, overpainted with a pair of bananas and additional grapes, Brumidi Corridors (West Corridor).

Fruit cluster after conservation, restored to the original mural with peppers, Brumidi Corridors (West Corridor).

Bananas in the Brumidi Corridors

Late 19th- and early 20th-century attempts to repair and restore the Brumidi Corridors resulted in overpainted surfaces that altered the character of the historic, mid-19th-century murals and changed many of Brumidi's original details. A conservator's trained eye often detects these stylistic or technical differences between overpaint and original work, even before testing the paint surfaces. In 2008, conservator Christy Cunningham-Adams observed that a pair of ripe bananas in the West Corridor looked out of proportion in a panel depicting bountiful clusters of fruit. She removed the layers of overpaint and discovered that the bananas had been a later addition to the mural. Brumidi's original painting, hidden under the bananas, depicted peppers, whose smaller size better suited the composition.

Most Americans had not seen a banana in the 1850s, when Brumidi and his team of artists painted the Brumidi Corridors. The 1876 Philadelphia Centennial Exposition officially introduced the fruit to the American public and offered fairgoers a chance to buy this exotic curiosity for 10 cents. In subsequent decades, the establishment of railroads and banana plantations, as well as improved shipping methods for this perishable commodity, made bananas so widely available that, by 1910, the littered peels were considered a public nuisance.

Cunningham-Adams speculates that a crack in the wall plaster near Brumidi's peppers may have resulted in a subsequent artist's painting over the repaired fissure, as well as the original peppers, with the longer and more "modern" bananas.

A putto before and after conservation, Brumidi Corridors (North Corridor).

Before conservation, overpaint gave the putto a cartoon-like appearance, *left*. The greater refinement of the original putto's face and modeled forms can be seen after conservation, *right*.

Left, top to bottom: **Groundhogs before, during, and after conservation, Brumidi Corridors (West Corridor).**

Conservators documented the restoration of this mural depicting a pair of groundhogs. Before treatment, *left top*, overpaint introduced teeth and heavily rimmed eyes. After removal of overpaint, *left center*, paint losses in the original mural are evident. The same detail is shown after careful inpainting of the paint losses, *left bottom*.

What is it like to work at such a close range on a painting?

Studying an artist's paintings as closely as conservation treatment requires certainly does allow us to develop an understanding of Brumidi's techniques and style. This familiarity makes it easier to discern alterations to the original artwork. We estimate that over the past 140 years, 6 major restoration campaigns have been carried out on the Brumidi Corridors' wall murals. Not every inch of surface was repainted in each campaign. Generally, the decorative detail was found with three layers of overpaint, while the backgrounds were repainted five to six times.

Because Brumidi's murals reference a well-established style, overpaint stands out to the trained eye if it has compromised the integrity of the artwork. For example, the fire-engine red frequently used as overpaint in the Brumidi Corridors looks incongruous because one would expect "Indian red" instead, a natural mineral color that was used since ancient Roman times in such instances.

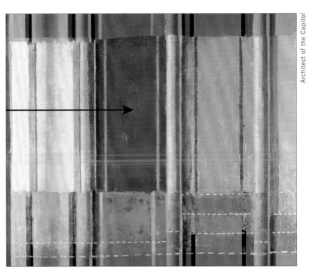

Architect of the Capitol

Conservation test exposure, Brumidi Corridors (North Corridor).

Removal of overpaint in a test window shows color and proportion changes introduced by later overpaint. Arrow indicates the traditional "Indian red" buried under fire-engine red overpaint.

Below: **Original surface versus color shift with five layers of overpaint, Brumidi Corridors (West Corridor).**

With each repainting of the murals, color shift gradually occurred. Here, overpaint eventually transformed the white and light pink background to a dull yellow and made the details darker, heavier, and uncharacteristic of Brumidi's original painting.

Architect of the Capitol

George W. Adams

Villa Arianna, Stabiae, Italy, ca. 80 B.C.

This example of ancient Roman wall painting shows the type of color palette, marbleizing, trompe l'oeil panels, and illusionistic architectural elements that Brumidi referenced in his mural designs for the Brumidi Corridors.

How did the traditions of antiquity influence the murals in the Brumidi Corridors?

The rich tradition of classical wall painting can be seen in the overall design layout, the decorative patterns, and many of the motifs in the Brumidi Corridors. The painting style and subjects fashioned by the ancient Romans influenced artists like Brumidi, who looked to antiquity and its revivals to embellish the walls and ceilings of contemporary public and private buildings.

In the third century B.C., the ancient Romans drew from Egyptian and Hellenistic traditions to develop a painting style for walls and ceilings that reflected the character and sophistication of their own culture. The ancient Romans used fresco painting to make plain surfaces appear to be constructed of costly materials and to create the illusion of greater space within interiors.

For nearly four centuries, ancient Roman wall painting flourished. Throughout its development, the wall painting used a formal layout of established wall divisions and a standardized color palette of primarily earth tones, as well as embellishments simulating marble or stone to integrate the painted decorations with the architectural structure.

Typically, wall murals in ancient Roman interiors were divided into three sections. The middle section, which was the largest, was divided vertically into rectangular panels that were outlined with flat bands of contrasting color. While the earliest designs depicted illusionistic architectural elements with elegant simplicity, the panels eventually became more elaborately painted with garlands of fruits and flowers, floating figures, inset landscapes, or complex architectural illusions. The lower section, or dado, and upper section, representing a cornice or frieze, were both treated with trompe l'oeil slabs of colorful marble or other stone.

The mural painting was executed with a light hand to keep the overall character lively and three-dimensional. The painting was characterized by a high level of technical skill and lent a distinct look to the interiors.

Mosaic of the Doves, Roman copy of the Greek mosaic attributed to Sosos (active 2nd century B.C.).

Brumidi's adaptation of the birds at a vessel, Brumidi Corridors (North Corridor).

The Doves of Pliny

Classical antiquity strongly influenced Brumidi's efforts in the Capitol, and his namesake corridors hold a witty reference to one of antiquity's most celebrated mosaics. The second-century B.C. floor mosaic, called the *Doves of Pliny*, was executed by the ancient Greek artist Sosos and depicted four birds perched on the rim of a water vessel. This subject permitted the artist to demonstrate his aptitude in creating artful illusions, such as reflections upon water, with mosaic *tesserae*, or tiles.

The dove mosaic was described in 77 A.D. by Roman natural historian Pliny the Elder in *Natural History*:

> A remarkable detail . . . is a dove, which is drinking and casts the shadow of its head on the water, while others are sunning and preening themselves on the brim of a large drinking vessel.
>
> (XXXVI.184)

The Greek mosaic described by Pliny, however, no longer exists. A Roman copy, believed to be a faithful replica of Sosos' original, was discovered in 1737 at Hadrian's Villa in Tivoli. When the Roman copy—called the *Mosaic of the Doves*—was discovered, it became immensely popular. As neoclassicism swept Europe in the 18th and early 19th centuries, copies of the dove mosaic flooded the markets. The image enjoyed such popularity that it was even replicated in jewelry for fashionable ladies.

As one of Rome's leading artists, Brumidi would have been well familiar with this traditional motif. Cleverly, Brumidi adapted the design of the renowned mosaic for use in the North Corridor of the Capitol by inserting American birds into the ancient formula. Copying the vessel and the birds' poses and shadows, Brumidi traded classical doves for American Robins and an Indigo Bunting.

Your description of ancient Roman wall painting calls to mind the murals in the Senate's first floor reception area, which have been transformed by your conservation efforts.

Yes, the Senate's first floor reception area shows how Brumidi integrated classical elements within a contemporary setting, although for many decades, overpaint concealed the extent of his artistry. These murals present Brumidi's reference to the earliest ancient Roman wall painting style, with primarily illusionistic architectural elements punctuated by occasional medallions of landscapes and animals.

Although the design was well balanced and in proportion to the lobby's architecture, the murals' apparent execution reflected little of the refinement of ancient Roman traditions. We suspected that this anomaly was due to overpaint that obscured Brumidi's original work and that changed the character of the entire decoration. The type of paint used was too shiny and dense to create any delicate illusion or pleasing effect. The panels' borders looked stiff, as if they had been painted using a yardstick to create straight edges instead of freehand. Furthermore, the drab brown color palette of the overpainted panels struck a discordant note, considering the vibrant palette typically associated with classical wall painting. Intriguingly, the panels' eight inset landscape medallions—linking New World imagery to the classical decorative scheme—were of such an obvious high quality that the absence of an aesthetic context of equal refinement and beauty made us very curious about what might be hidden beneath the overpaint.

What did you eventually find when you restored the Senate reception area's wall and ceiling murals?

As we began to remove overpaint from the wall panels in the Senate reception area, brightly colored and three-dimensional effects emerged. Brumidi's refined trompe l'oeil techniques made the panels appear to be composed of inset plaques or slabs of colored stone surrounded by molding. The alternating colors of celadon and salmon, punctuated with bands of "Indian red," bore strong resemblance to the classical prototypes that inspired them.

Cunningham-Adams

Left: **Senate reception area before restoration, Brumidi Corridors.**

Darkened incrementally by numerous repaintings, the reception area developed a predominantly brown, grim appearance.

Opposite: **Restored Senate reception area, Brumidi Corridors.**

A combination of conservation and replication of the wall and ceiling murals reinstated the original bright colors and the dimensionality of the trompe l'oeil panels. The restoration effort has helped reconnect Brumidi's designs with ancient Roman prototypes.

Restoration of this area has helped enhance our understanding of Brumidi's well-planned design for the interiors of the Senate wing. Once restored, the murals in the Senate reception area began to complement the décor in the adjoining corridors. Overpaint had undermined the subtle but important details, such as the palette, succinct brushwork, and high quality of execution, that Brumidi skillfully employed to unite very different spaces and styles in the Brumidi Corridors.

Conservation has helped inform our understanding of Brumidi's wall and ceiling murals. What additional design elements have you explored?

In 2001, after spending several years focused on the wall murals in the Brumidi Corridors, we investigated earlier finishes on the cast-iron window enframements. The enframements' existing cream-colored paint was incongruous with the types of historic effects that would traditionally accompany a decoration like the one Brumidi created for the corridors. We wondered if paring away the overpaint would reveal something more relevant.

With extreme care, under a microscope at 10x, we revealed some sophisticated faux marble in a one-square-foot test area. Our exposure found a grey-colored coating applied directly to the cast-iron enframement. A previous study indicated that this was a primer applied at the factory. The next layer that we uncovered was a pinkish-mauve color that I believe functioned as a chromatic base and preparation for the marbleizing. When we revealed an off-white layer with grey patches and bluish-grey veining, the effect of simulated marble immediately became apparent. The faux marble matches genuine marble used throughout the Capitol, particularly in the columns in the Senate's adjoining East Entry. More testing and analysis will be necessary to complete these promising initial findings.

In our continued research, we studied the dark green, overpainted cornices in the corridors and then replicated the earliest color that testing found—a pale grey color that gives the cornices the appearance of natural stone. Similarly, an exposure on the plain pinkish tan-colored wall sections surrounding the Brumidi Corridors' decorative panels revealed marks that could be intended to depict sandstone. I hope that future study will tell us the whole story about the trompe l'oeil effects used throughout the Brumidi Corridors. The frequent references to stone would considerably broaden our appreciation of Brumidi's overall design and link the Capitol's decoration even more strongly to historic prototypes.

Architect of the Capitol

Conservation test exposures of cast-iron window enframement, Brumidi Corridors (Patent Corridor).

The earliest layers of paint appear to have created a marble effect, seen in the top exposure. Nearly 25 layers of overpaint on the enframement covered the marble effect.

Discovery of trompe l'oeil ceiling, conservation test exposure, Brumidi Corridors (East Entry).

Overpaint concealed the nuanced faux marble and trompe l'oeil anthemia pattern and drastically altered the once-elegant appearance of the East Entry.

You recently made a particularly thrilling and important discovery while conducting conservation testing in the Senate's East Entry—is it the discovery of a lifetime?

Our recent discovery in the East Entry certainly seemed like a reward for a decade of patience! The East Entry's dull, mustard-colored ceiling had bothered me for years as an unsuitable companion to the marble columns that adorn this formal entrance to the Senate wing of the Capitol. The marble is a classic white stone shot through with splashes of dark blue and charcoal gray, but the ceiling has been a lackluster expanse of mustard paint for as long as anyone can remember.

Finally, in 2010, we performed overpaint removal tests. Our patience was amply rewarded. We discovered that underneath the dull, mustard-colored ceiling was a striking faux marble that made the ceiling resemble the real marble columns in the entry. Not only did the ceiling appear to be constructed of marble, the arches in the dome-vaulted ceiling also looked as if they had been carved with ornate bands of anthemia, a classical border motif with palmette, or fan-shaped, leaves. The trompe l'oeil ceiling was a remarkable find and offered a dazzling testimony to the range of skills of Brumidi and his assistant artists. Among Brumidi's many talents was his ability to connect his designs to the architecture of the Capitol. With this thrilling discovery of the trompe l'oeil ceiling, we are now able to envision the original resplendent and impressive entranceway in the Senate wing.

Nearly 20 years ago, you embarked on the conservation of the Brumidi Corridors, and still you are deeply inspired and passionate about your work. What do you find most meaningful about the conservation you have accomplished at the Capitol?

It is both exhilarating and deeply moving to be a part of this important restoration project and to see the types of aesthetic details that we are recovering through conservation. The association between the U.S. Capitol and classical traditions thousands of years old has been reawakened, and visitors, scholars, and curators can now appreciate the many historic elements that Brumidi brought to the Capitol. It has been important to restore the Capitol interiors to their original refinement, so that the artistic adornment of the building can once again complement the architectural quality. Although our work here is not complete, what we have seen so far promises much.

Part of the Brumidi Corridors conservation team for the past 15 years, Laurie Timm is shown retouching the trompe l'oeil borders in the Zodiac Corridor. After the challenge of removing overpaint, this phase of recovering the original aesthetic character is the conservator's reward.

Ancient vessel with fruit, Brumidi Corridors (North Corridor).

Reinterpreting a Classic

The design for the most prominent section of the Brumidi Corridors was inspired by the Vatican Palace's loggia—a virtuoso Renaissance interpretation of ancient Roman ornamentation. In the early 1500s, the Italian Renaissance artist Raphael studied ancient Roman motifs, including those discovered in 1480 at Emperor Nero's palace, and incorporated them in his murals for the Vatican's 213-foot-long arcade, or loggia, just outside the pope's private apartment. The loggia's iconic decoration had an enormous impact across Europe and brought many classical wall painting techniques and designs back into vogue. The scrolling vines, birds, animals, floral wreaths, and trompe l'oeil panels decorating the Brumidi Corridors derive from the distinctive Vatican murals. In the late 1700s, discovery of ancient Roman sites like Pompeii and Herculaneum revitalized classical styles and fueled the neoclassical period, during which Brumidi trained and worked. Brumidi absorbed characteristics from ancient Roman, Renaissance, and neoclassical styles into his repertoire.

The imprint of Brumidi's own time and place can be felt in his murals at the U.S. Capitol. Most notably, Brumidi assimilated American iconography into the classical framework and used a color palette that worked in concert with the Capitol's 1850s Minton floor tiles. Ancient vessels overflowing with North American fruit, an allegorical figure of Authority customized with a tablet inscribed "Constitution and Union," and *scudi*, or shields, patterned with American stripes are just a few of the traditional motifs Brumidi adapted to reflect the contemporary interests of his adopted country.

Architect of the Capitol

Landscape medallion (detail), Brumidi Corridors.

Brumidi's landscape medallions relate to the federally sponsored *Pacific Railroad Report* and depict scenes from the American West, such as this view of Mount Baker in Washington State.

The "Most Practicable" Route

Brumidi's Landscapes and the Transcontinental Railroad

Amy Elizabeth Burton

For 150 years, senators, dignitaries, and visitors to the U.S. Capitol have bustled past 8 landscape medallions prominently located in the reception area of the Brumidi Corridors on the first floor of the Senate wing. For most of this time, very little was understood about these scenes of rivers and mountains. The locations depicted in the landscapes and any relevance the paintings once held had long faded from memory. The art of the Capitol is deeply rooted in symbolism and themes that reflect national pride, which strongly suggested that the medallions' significance extended beyond their decorative value. Ultimately, a breakthrough in scholarship identified the long-forgotten source of the eight landscapes and reconnected them to their historical context: a young nation exploring and uniting a vast continent, as well as a great national issue that was part of this American narrative—the first transcontinental railroad.

Starting in 1857, the Brumidi Corridors in the newly constructed Senate wing of the Capitol buzzed with artistic activity. Development of the mural designs for the Senate's lobbies and halls fell to artist Constantino Brumidi, under the watchful eye of Montgomery C. Meigs, supervising engineer of the Capitol extension. Both men were deeply invested in imbuing the art of the Capitol with iconography that expressed the national character. Meigs, an accomplished engineer, was also keen to have Brumidi depict new technologies that conferred civic benefit and economic development. Murals portraying inventions in agriculture and industry, innovations in transportation, and the laying of the transatlantic cable appear with great frequency throughout the building.

From roughly 1857 to 1861, Brumidi and his team of artists decorated the expansive Brumidi Corridors with Brumidi's designs, while one floor above, the Senate deliberated about the building of the nation's first transcontinental railroad. This key issue would occupy the minds of legislators and the American public for close to two decades in the mid-19th century.

Recent research has revealed that Brumidi reflected this pressing national concern when he created the eight landscape medallions in the Senate wing. The scenes Brumidi depicted are some of the very pictures of the American West recorded during the 1853–54 federal expeditions to survey routes for a transcontinental railroad.[1]

Top: *Mount Baker & Cascade Range*, lithograph from a sketch by John Mix Stanley, *Pacific Railroad Report*, Volume 12.

Bottom: Landscape medallion, Brumidi Corridors.

Top: *Cape Horn–Columbia River*, lithograph from a sketch by John Mix Stanley, *Pacific Railroad Report*, Volume 12.

Bottom: Landscape medallion, Brumidi Corridors.

Brumidi's landscapes, which closely resemble the *Pacific Railroad Report* illustrations, were evidently inspired by this mid–19th century publication.

The survey's official report, authorized by Congress, was published between 1855 and 1861 as a 12-volume set with a name as ambitious as the rail project itself: *Reports of Explorations and Surveys, to Ascertain the Most Practicable and Economical Route for a Railroad from the Mississippi River to the Pacific Ocean, Made under the Direction of the Secretary of War in 1853–4.* The *Pacific Railroad Report* is considered the high-water mark in mapping and documenting trans-Mississippi America before the Civil War and is a monumental record of the resources, scenery, and character of the American West.

The *Pacific Railroad Report* was generously illustrated. To help inform the decisions of lawmakers in Congress regarding the "most practicable" route for the future railroad, artists accompanied the survey expeditions and depicted the terrain of potential rail routes. Brumidi's eight

---

The medallions can now be identified as depicting specific geographic locations and can be understood in the context of the vital exploration and survey of the West for the proposed transcontinental railroad.

---

oval landscapes in the Capitol appear to be directly modeled on the *Pacific Railroad Report*'s illustrations. Brumidi slightly altered certain details, perhaps to accommodate differences in format (rectangular in the source material versus oval in the medallion murals) or to visually balance the compositions of the eight individual landscapes, which are set in pairs on opposing walls. Despite minor differences between the illustrations and medallions, Brumidi's landscapes clearly take inspiration from this important mid-19th-century publication. The medallions can now be identified as depicting specific geographic locations and can be understood in the context of the vital exploration and survey of the West for the proposed transcontinental railroad.

Landscape medallion panel, Brumidi Corridors.

Brumidi's landscape paintings feature prominently in the wall murals that he designed around 1861.

Hudson Bay Mill (detail), lithograph from a sketch by John Mix Stanley, *Pacific Railroad Report*, Volume 12.

As early as the 1820s, the Hudson's Bay Company operated saw and grist mills to serve nearby Fort Colville in what is now Washington State. The Pacific railroad surveyors documented the grist mill and purchased flour as they passed through the territory in 1853.

Landscape medallion (detail), Brumidi Corridors.

Brumidi based his landscape on the *Pacific Railroad Report* lithograph, *opposite page*. He copied specific details, such as the two loose planks near the mill, although he reversed the position of the fallen branch in the foreground.

The saga of the transcontinental railroad, including the historic 1853–54 survey, lends a provocative undercurrent to the seemingly gentle rivers in Brumidi's paintings. During the early 19th century, transportation in America was slow, difficult, unreliable, and often dangerous. Modes of transportation evolved from rivers and canals to roads, turnpikes, and railroads. As "railroad fever" spread through the East and Midwest, Congress quickly recognized the need to unite the nation's two coastlines with a railroad. From the early 1840s until passage of the Pacific Railway Act of 1862, Congress grappled with how to survey, fund, and build the railroad. It was indeed a project of daunting magnitude—an engineering endeavor that needed to overcome the vast plains, trackless deserts, and formidable mountain ranges that spanned two-thirds of the continent. Building the transcontinental railroad would be one of the greatest technological feats of the century, and construction of the railroad was estimated in 1859 to cost $100 million, a sum calculated at "one third of the entire surplus products of the United States."[2] Congress would also have to determine the constitutionality of the federal government's involvement in building the railroad and to define the extent and character of the aid Congress could rightfully extend to the proposed work.

With the end of the Mexican-American War and the discovery of gold in California in 1848, western settlement, travel, and trade, as well as defense of the nation's two coastlines, became increasingly vital concerns for legislators. Support for a transcontinental railroad ran strong, but the issue of which route the railroad should follow and the resulting competition of political interests led to stalemate. The difficult issue of states and slavery further complicated the debate, and in the volatile political environment of the 1850s, neither the anti-slavery North nor the pro-slavery South was willing to accept a compromise rail route. Northerners suggested a route along the 47th and 49th parallels. Senator Thomas Hart Benton of Missouri advocated a central route

between the 37th and 39th parallels. Secretary of War Jefferson Davis backed a more southern route. In March of 1853, with the contentious political dust swirling, the Thirty-second Congress approved the provisions of the Army Appropriation Act and directed Secretary Davis to dispatch survey teams to explore four possible east-to-west rail routes to the Pacific Ocean. Each route roughly followed specific latitudes. Two months after Congress approved the measure, the railroad survey expeditions were underway.

Starting in 1855, the reports generated by the survey expeditions began to roll off the press, leather bound for Congress. Speaking on the Senate floor in 1859, Senator James Harlan of Iowa, who lent his voice to pass the railroad bills, reminded his colleagues of their duty to study the publication and reach "an enlightened decision":

I find that Congress passed a law, approved March 3, 1853, appropriating $150,000, and May 31, 1854, appropriating $40,000 more, and August 5, 1854, $150,000 in addition, to be expended, under the direction of the Secretary of War, in an exploration and survey of all the routes then proposed. In all, $340,000 have been withdrawn from the Treasury of the United States, by Congress, for the purpose of securing the requisite information. These laws have been faithfully executed. The corps of engineers, appointed on the various routes, have laboriously performed their duties. They have made their reports to their superior, the Secretary of War, and they have been ordered to be printed, and eight large quarto volumes have been laid on the desks of Senators.[3]

Because of the national and political significance of the proposed railroad, the *Pacific Railroad Report* generated a great deal of interest at the time it was published. Print runs for the dozen volumes ranged from 21,000 to 53,000, and the publication was discussed in newspapers and reviewed in contemporary periodicals. The cost of the report's production reflects its importance.

In a period of 5 years, the federal government spent nearly $1.3 million to produce the 12 volumes. Brumidi was certainly sensitive to the *Pacific Railroad Report's* salience to his congressional patrons, but the publication also offered the artist unique views of the landscapes, flora, and fauna of the West before photography made such imagery widely available. Prior to painting the landscape medallions, Brumidi used volume 10 of the *Pacific Railroad Report,* issued in 1859, to help him depict birds in the Brumidi Corridors that were native to the American West.

The specific material that Brumidi selected from the *Pacific Railroad Report* for his painted landscapes is worth noting. The artists on the railroad survey illustrated mountains, passes, and other distinctive terrain that would challenge engineers and require exceptional outlays of funds from backers of the railroad construction. The artists also carefully documented rivers, for those were the convenient and economical routes along which railroads were frequently built.[4] Brumidi eschewed the dramatic scenes of canyons, waterfalls,

Map of Routes for a Pacific Railroad, by G.K. Warren, *Pacific Railroad Report*, Volume 11, lithograph, 1855.

and herds of buffalo stretching across the horizon—illustrations that offered copious material had Brumidi wished to portray the grand terrain of the American West. Instead, he favored tranquil river scenes. Seven out of the eight landscapes in Brumidi's medallions illustrate free-flowing rivers with distant mountains punctuating the backgrounds. Today, the river scenes in the Senate look picturesque; in Brumidi's time, rivers provided crucial passageways through difficult lands and supplied water needed for crew, passengers, live cargo, and steam engines.

Interestingly, Brumidi did not give equal treatment in his murals to the four proposed east-to-west routes

Coeur d'Alene Mission, St. Ignatius River, lithograph from a sketch by John Mix Stanley, *Pacific Railroad Report*, Volume 12.

Catholic missionaries and members of the Coeur d'Alene tribe built the Coeur d'Alene Mission church between 1850 and 1853. It is the oldest standing building in Idaho.

Landscape medallion, Brumidi Corridors.

The composition and details in Brumidi's landscape show the direct influence of the *Pacific Railroad Report* lithograph.

that were detailed in the *Pacific Railroad Report*. Three-fourths of Brumidi's medallions depict landscapes from the northern survey, bracketed by the 47th and 49th parallels. During his 25-year career at the Capitol, Brumidi shied away from politics or controversy (perhaps a result of his political imprisonment in Italy from 1851 to 1852), so it is unlikely that this weighting towards one particular route was an overt political statement. An explanation may, in part, be as simple as convenience: the volume that Brumidi used for the majority

Tragically, three separate fires would destroy Stanley's life work and deny him a place as a nationally recognized artist by future generations.

of his landscapes was the most generously illustrated of the set, and it offered Brumidi many handsome illustrations from which to choose. Volume 12 of the *Pacific Railroad Report* included 70 landscape plates and was published in 1860. It was shortly thereafter, in 1861, that Brumidi and two assistant artists were hired to complete the area with the landscape medallions.

The influential volume 12 was largely illustrated by the expedition artist John Mix Stanley. Stanley's illustrations inspired six of Brumidi's eight medallions. Brumidi also adapted the work of artists Richard H. Kern from volume 2 and Baron F.W. von Egloffstein from volume 11. These artists, who accompanied the Pacific railroad expeditions, recorded pencil sketches while in the field. They then rendered the sketches into watercolors, ultimately printed as color lithographs, or a few as steel engravings, when the final report was prepared. Detailed narrative accounts of the expeditions frequently accompanied the illustrations. The singular experiences of these expedition artists, whose work Brumidi preserved for posterity in the Senate's murals, hint at the complex flavor of the American frontier in the early 1850s.

The expedition artist John Mix Stanley was an established figure in Washington, D.C., art circles in the mid-1850s. Tragically, three separate fires would destroy Stanley's life work and deny him a place as a nationally recognized artist by future generations. Even before Brumidi began work in the corridors, Montgomery C. Meigs was aware of Stanley. Meigs' journal, a valuable source of information about the commissioning of art for the Capitol extension, briefly mentions that, on October 22, 1856, a mutual acquaintance recommended that Stanley paint an "Indian scene" for a committee room in the Capitol.[5]

Top: **Bois de Sioux River**, lithograph from a sketch by John Mix Stanley, *Pacific Railroad Report*, Volume 12.

Bottom: Landscape medallion, Brumidi Corridors.

According to the narrative account, the expedition party sat down at 11 p.m. on June 28, 1853, to a supper of coffee, ducks, and several catfish weighing 12 to 20 pounds each.

Lieut. Grover's Despatch—Return of Governor Stevens to Fort Benton, lithograph from a sketch by John Mix Stanley, *Pacific Railroad Report*, Volume 12.

This scene depicts a small exploratory party that included Stevens, Stanley (seated and sketching), an Indian chief escort, and an interpreter. The illustration provides a glimpse of the daily experience of the expedition parties.

Stanley's body of work documented the culture and landscapes of the American frontier. The artist's 12-year journey through the West began in 1839, prior to extensive settlement of the land. Stanley joined various expeditions and captured the West with his portraits of Native Americans and landscapes. Stanley's intimate knowledge and personal experience of the American frontier were unrivalled. Only a handful of his paintings survive today, but Stanley was prolific, and his work was widely acclaimed in his time.

In 1852, Stanley displayed 150 paintings at the Smithsonian Institution and tried to interest members of Congress in purchasing the collection as the foundation of a national gallery. The Senate Committee on Indian Affairs recommended the collection's purchase for $19,200, and the Senate debated the acquisition of Stanley's paintings. Despite the support of Senator John Weller of California and Senator Isaac Walker of Wisconsin, the purchase was defeated when it came to a vote in March 1853.[6] The collection remained at the Smithsonian and grew to over 200 of Stanley's paintings, before a fire at the Smithsonian in 1865 destroyed the collection. A second fire at P.T. Barnum's American Museum consumed additional paintings. After Stanley's death, a fire at his studio destroyed field sketches and later work—in all, an irreparable cultural loss to the nation.

Thankfully, a sampling of Stanley's documentation of the frontier West can still be found in the *Pacific*

Herd of Bison, near Lake Jessie, lithograph from a sketch by John Mix Stanley, *Pacific Railroad Report,* Volume 12.

Expedition artists witnessed exceptional scenes from the frontier. According to the report's account, buffalo were hunted twice a year to procure dried meat, tongues, skins, and "pemmican," a mixture of dried buffalo meat, fat, and berries developed by Native Americans that proved popular with westward explorers and expansionists.

Railroad Report. Joining the railroad survey at its onset in 1853, Stanley accompanied Isaac Stevens, first governor of Washington Territory, on the northern route and was the highest paid member of Stevens' expedition.[7] In volume 12, Stevens chronicled the arduous and fascinating experiences of his expedition party—from daily tasks and hardships to exceptional encounters with nature and interactions with Native Americans. On July 10, 1853, Stanley and Stevens witnessed the vast herds of buffalo populating the western plains prior to the railroad. Stanley sketched the scene, and Stevens recorded: "About five miles from camp we ascended to the top of a high hill, and for a great distance ahead every square mile seemed to have a herd of buffalo upon it. . . . I had heard of the myriads of these animals inhabiting these plains, but I could not realize the truth of these accounts till to-day, when they surpassed anything I could have imagined from the accounts which I had received. The reader will form a better idea of this scene from the accompanying sketch, taken by Mr. Stanley on the ground, than from any description."[8] A reporter who interviewed Stanley would later add emphasis, "The artist in sketching this scene, stood on an elevation in advance of the foreground, whence, with a spy-glass, he could see fifteen miles in any direction, and *yet* he saw not the limit of the herd."[9] This sketch is one of the few extant scenes of its kind recorded in frontier times.[10]

Life as an expedition artist had perils to accompany its thrills. One of Brumidi's landscape medallion paintings serves as a reminder of the danger these expedition artists faced in the line of duty. Its corresponding lithograph, *Sangre de Cristo Pass*, was based on a scene completed by Stanley after the untimely death of the original artist, Richard H. Kern. Kern was one of three brothers with artistic skills who served on expeditions. Both Kern and a brother were killed by Native American Indians in separate incidents.

On October 25, 1853, Kern and 10 other men left their main party and escorted Captain John W. Gunnison, leader of the railroad's southern expedition along the 38th and 39th parallels, to survey Sevier Lake in Utah. Ute Indians ambushed the group. Gunnison was pierced with 15 arrows; Kern and 2 other men in the party were killed as well. Measures were taken to recover the instruments, field notes, and Kern's sketch book taken by the Indians. Fortunately, "all the notes, most of the instruments, and several of the arms lost" were reclaimed.[11] The remains of the slain were located and given "the solemn rite of burial."[12] It was Kern's field sketches that Stanley later used to prepare some of the lithograph scenes found in volume 2.

Baron F.W. von Egloffstein, the third artist whose survey illustrations are represented in Brumidi's landscape

Sangre de Cristo Pass, lithograph from a sketch by John Mix Stanley and Richard H. Kern, *Pacific Railroad Report*, Volume 2, *top*; and Brumidi's landscape, *bottom*, were based on a scene sketched in the field by Kern, who was killed by Ute Indians during the expedition.

Franklin Valley, an engraving from a sketch by F.W. Egloffstein, *Pacific Railroad Report*, Volume 11, *top*, served as the model for Brumidi's medallion, *bottom*. Brumidi did not include figures when he translated the lithographs into medallion paintings.

medallions, was a Prussian-born topographical engineer. Egloffstein had survived Colonel John C. Frémont's ill-fated expedition through the Rocky Mountains in 1853–54. (Frémont's sponsor was his father-in-law, Senator Thomas Hart Benton, who was determined to prove that the railroad should run through the central route.)

The connection between the Senate's murals and the federally sponsored Pacific Railroad Report *now brings a rich and colorful tone to Brumidi's landscapes.*

After serving as Frémont's artist under challenging conditions, Egloffstein arrived "half-dead" in Salt Lake City. Undeterred, he joined the Pacific railroad expeditions as a replacement for the slain Kern. Brumidi paired one of Egloffstein's landscapes from volume 11 with Kern's landscape on one of the Senate reception area's walls.

The connection between the Senate's murals and the federally sponsored *Pacific Railroad Report* now brings a rich and colorful tone to Brumidi's landscapes. How many years, however, had the landscapes languished, their identity and historical context forgotten? Even as Brumidi's paints were drying on the walls—on murals that celebrated the beauty and grace of America's scenery and anticipated the future railroad—the nation was forced to turn its attention to the Civil War. In 1861, following secession and withdrawal of the southern bloc (and with a southern rail route no longer an option), Congress speedily approved a route that was advantageous to northern interests.

Brumidi had finished his landscape medallions in the Brumidi Corridors when Congress finally passed legislation for the railroad in June 1862. President Lincoln signed the Pacific Railway Act that July, but when he did, the route for the proposed transcontinental railroad did not correspond with any of the "practicable routes" whose illustrations appear in the Brumidi Corridors. While the *Pacific Railroad Report*

"Convalescent Soldiers Passing through Washington to Join Their Regiments" (detail), *Harper's Weekly*, engraving, November 15, 1862.

The advent of the Civil War influenced Congress' decision about the route for the transcontinental railroad. The proposed southern routes were eliminated from consideration.

helped identify geographical passages through which future railroads would one day be constructed, the report had failed to provide a "conclusive solution" to Congress for the first transcontinental railroad.[13] So much had changed for the nation since Congress had initially dispatched the survey teams nine years earlier.

The *Pacific Railroad Report* quickly fell into obscurity, rendered obsolete by newer topographical engineering studies and by advancing technologies. Photography in the 1860s brought a new and more accurate way than an artist's rendering to document the West and provide imagery of distant lands. These lands, in fact, became much more accessible in 1869, when the nation's first transcontinental railroad was completed, finally linking the East and West. The identity of the landscapes and the meaning behind Brumidi's medallions faded with their source of inspiration, the *Pacific Railroad Report*.

When Brumidi passed away in 1880, he left a number of paintings and oil studies to his son Laurence. One of these paintings was an oval landscape of a mountain scene, possibly a preliminary study for a medallion in the Brumidi Corridors.[14] The painting's whereabouts are unknown today. What we do now know is that the eight gentle landscapes Brumidi included in the Senate's first floor murals capture a slice of the era in which they were painted. The once-enigmatic landscapes thus take their place with the other symbolic and thematically relevant art in the Capitol and help commemorate the people, places, and innovations that so greatly shaped the nation.

Crossing the Bitter Root [sic], lithograph from a sketch by John Mix Stanley, *Pacific Railroad Report*, Volume 12.

Landscape medallion, Brumidi Corridors.

The inclusion of the footbridge in the medallion seems to be a case of artistic license. According to the narrative account, the expedition party encountered Nez Perce Indians riding "splendid" horses to a hunt. Fallen timber on land made the journey "tedious." The party crossed the river at 8 a.m. on October 9, 1853, and made no mention of a bridge.

Steam locomotive, detail from *Liberty, Peace, Plenty, War,* fresco, 1869.

Locomotives in Brumidi's Frescoes

The development of the steam locomotive in the 19th century revolutionized the American way of life, and nothing embodied technological progress in the eye of the nation as powerfully as the "Iron Horse." Rail lines covered the East and Midwest by the first half of the century, and in 1869, the first transcontinental railroad—a true engineering marvel—united America's coasts.

Brumidi's frescoes in the Capitol frequently reference technology. The billowing plumes of white vapor or dark smoke that issue from his locomotives and ships announce the power of their steam-driven engines. Of the handful of locomotives in Brumidi's allegorical frescoes, the Senate Reception Room's *Liberty, Peace, Plenty, War* provides the most recognizable example. Painted in 1869 from a sketch Brumidi had created nearly 10 years earlier, the locomotive is flanked by the caduceus of commerce, bears the number "31," and is crowned by a wood-burning smokestack. The wheel arrangement identifies it as a 4-4-0, a model widely known as the "American Standard," with its bright colors, highly decorative brass work, hand-built wooden cabs, and pilot, or "cowcatcher."

The 4-4-0 locomotive's popularity extended from the 1840s to the late 19th century. This model was used locally on the Baltimore and Ohio's Washington Branch. Two celebrated 4-4-0s included the Central Pacific Railroad's wood-burning Jupiter and the Union Pacific's coal-burning No. 119. The two trains met at Promontory Summit in the Utah territory on May 10, 1869, for the Golden Spike ceremony commemorating completion of the first transcontinental railroad.

The Battle of Lexington (detail), oil on canvas sketch, ca. 1857.

Brumidi's artistic talent and strong compositions are beautifully expressed in his small preparatory sketches.

A Collection of Brumidi Sketches

ARTISTIC PROCESS AND PATRIOTIC ENDEAVOR

Diane K. Skvarla

Five important oil sketches by Constantino Brumidi recently made their way back to the United States Capitol after more than a century's absence. Painted in the 1850s, the sketches reflect the foresight and efforts of several key figures: Montgomery C. Meigs, the supervising engineer of the Capitol extension who envisioned a building filled with art inspired by nationalist themes; Brumidi, the artist who applied his significant talents to ornamenting the Capitol with murals and to carrying out Meigs' vision; and the Macomb family, the civic-minded stewards who kept this distinctive collection of sketches intact for over 100 years. Brumidi painted the scenes in preparation for some of his most impressive frescoes in the Capitol, and a comparison of these small-scale works with the large-scale frescoes provides an intimate and insightful look at Brumidi's creative process and classical training.

Between 1855 and 1859, during his early years at the Capitol, Brumidi executed the five small oil on canvas sketches now owned by the Senate and House of Representatives. The collection included one sketch that Brumidi painted in preparation for his first fresco in the Capitol for the House Agriculture Committee Room, three for the Senate Committee on Military Affairs and Militia Room, and one for the Senate Reception Room. These sketches resulted from the collaboration between Brumidi and Meigs, and the success of this partnership, along with Meigs' oversight of the process, ultimately enabled the Macomb family to acquire the collection in the late 19th century.

Montgomery Meigs was a captain in the Army Corps of Engineers when Secretary of War Jefferson Davis appointed him in 1853 to the post of supervising engineer of the Capitol extension. Meigs was responsible for constructing the Capitol's additions and for negotiating contracts and hiring workers.

Meigs' role was to build spacious new quarters for the Senate and House of Representatives, and ultimately, to construct a massive cast-iron dome for the Capitol, but he involved himself in embellishing the building as well. An astute administrator and civil engineer, Meigs also took great pride and pleasure in the arts. He frequented galleries, met and corresponded with artists, and read about the art and architecture of the

Between 1855 and 1859, during his early years at the Capitol, Brumidi executed the five small oil on canvas sketches now owned by the Senate and House of Representatives.

world. This lifelong interest, as well as his desire to commemorate America through the arts and make the Capitol a great national monument, influenced Meigs' ambitious plans for the building.[1]

U.S. Senate Collection

"Birdseye View of the City of Washington, with the Capitol in the Foreground," *The Illustrated London News*, engraving, May 25, 1861.
Brumidi's arrival at the Capitol coincided with the expansion of the building.

Meigs intended that the art of the Capitol inspire patriotic pride. He commissioned murals, paintings, and sculpture to illustrate the nation's history, values, and achievements. Meigs explained his vision for the Capitol's public art: "Although an engineer and 'nothing more' I have some feeling for art, some little acquaintance with its principles and its precepts and a very strong desire to use the opportunities & the influence which my position, as directing head of this great work, gives me for the advancement of art in this country."[2] Brumidi echoed Meigs' convictions. The artist reportedly proclaimed: "My one ambition and my daily prayer is that I may live long enough to make beautiful the Capitol of the one country on earth in which there is liberty."[3] Brumidi's patriotic sentiment and artistic skill, combined with Meigs' emphasis on America's history and symbolism, created the distinctive art seen in the Capitol today.

On December 28, 1854, Constantino Brumidi came to the Capitol seeking employment and was introduced to Montgomery Meigs. Impressed by the artist's credentials, Meigs gave Brumidi the opportunity to demonstrate his talent for painting fresco. Meigs assigned Brumidi the room intended for the House Agricultural Committee and, for the fresco, chose the theme of the Roman leader Cincinnatus called from the plow to serve his country.[4] Brumidi was familiar with the story, having previously painted a lunette of the subject in Rome.[5] Brumidi created a small oil on canvas sketch of the scene for Meigs' approval. The preparatory study pleased Meigs, who praised Brumidi's skill in drawing, composition, and coloring.[6] The success of the sketch and the resulting fresco, *Calling of Cincinnatus from the Plow*, marked the beginning of Brumidi's 25-year career at the United States Capitol.

After completion of the Cincinnatus fresco in 1855, Meigs directed Brumidi to create several small oil sketches in preparation for the frescoes in the Senate Committee on Military Affairs and Militia Room.[7]

Collection of the U.S. House of Representatives

Sketch for *Calling of Cincinnatus from the Plow*, oil on canvas, 1855.

Brumidi prepared this oil on canvas sketch for his first Capitol fresco. The lower scene, depicting an allegorical image of Agriculture with Native American figures, was never executed in fresco.

As Meigs contemplated the decorative scheme for this room in 1856, illustrator Felix Darley advised: "The best subjects for the room of the committee on 'military affairs' would be scenes from the Revolution when Washington or his principal generals could be introduced, such as the Storming of Stony Point, the Battle of Trenton &c."[8] Brumidi originally painted three preparatory sketches for the room's five lunettes, with each of the sketches illustrating two different battle scenes. Two of the scenes, from two of the sketches, were almost immediately translated into fresco: *Death*

of General Wooster, 1777 and *The Battle of Lexington.* These are some of Brumidi's strongest images of American history.[9] The pictures poignantly illustrate the turmoil and conflict of the Revolutionary War. Brumidi designed the scenes to fit the lunettes' proportions, and the completed frescoes are the focal points of the room.

In keeping with the traditional practices of his classical training, Brumidi frequently prepared oil sketches before he began work on his murals at the Capitol. In fresco painting, it is necessary to develop

U.S. Senate Collection

General Mercer's Death by Bayonet Stroke and Storming of Stony Point, General Wayne Wounded in the Head, Carried into the Fort, oil on canvas sketch, ca. 1857.

In preparation for his frescoes in the Senate Military Affairs and Militia Committee Room, Brumidi painted three oil sketches, each depicting two scenes. Only the lower image of this sketch was rendered in fresco.

the composition beforehand, as the medium does not easily permit experimentation or reworking. Often, Brumidi's first step was to analyze the room's architectural space and make a pencil drawing that showed the planned frescoes in relation to the overall decorative scheme of the room. He then prepared small-scale color sketches of each scene in oil or watercolor, which he submitted for approval. Next, Brumidi enlarged the preparatory sketch on paper to the exact scale of the proposed fresco and placed the resulting paper cartoon on the wall over the area to be painted. He transferred the outlines of the image to the wet mortar through a variety of techniques and used the preparatory sketch as reference when painting the actual fresco.[10] While the sketches were only the prelude to the frescoes, Brumidi included in the sketches all of the essential elements for the final murals and created well-constructed compositions and beautifully rendered scenes.

With minor exceptions, the frescoes are faithful to Brumidi's preparatory oil sketches. The differences between the two reflect the nature of the two mediums, the contrast in scale, and the function that each work served.

Architect of the Capitol

Senate Military Affairs and Militia Committee Room, ca. 1895.

Brumidi's frescoes encircling the room (now part of the Senate Appropriations Committee suite) reflect the original occupant and pay tribute to American military history.

Death of General Wooster, 1777, fresco, 1858.

General Wooster at Ridgefield Mortally Wounded, Is Carried out of the Field and The Americans at Sagg [sic] *Harbor Burned Twelve Brigs and Sloops, and* [illegible] *Bringing with Him Many Prisoners*, oil on canvas sketch, ca. 1857.

Oil painting as a medium allows spontaneity and elaboration, as the artist can rework the paint and can change or add details. The ability to use dynamic brushwork and an underlying dark ground lends a sense of action and drama to Brumidi's oil sketches. In contrast, the brushwork in Brumidi's frescoes is more studied and precise, as reworking the wet mortar of fresco muddies the surface and causes the image to lose clarity. Since the fresco medium has a limited color palette, as only certain pigments can withstand the alkalinity of the mortar, this further creates a dissimilar appearance between Brumidi's preliminary studies and finished frescoes. The range in scale of Brumidi's oil sketches and frescoes introduces yet another variable in the visual impact of the two media. The sketches were intended to be seen at a close range and allowed Brumidi to conceptualize the subject matter, overall composition, relationship of the figures to each other and to the background, use of light and shade, and coloring. Finally, in evaluating the oil sketches and frescoes, it is important to remember that the sketches were only preparatory paintings created quickly; they were never intended to be viewed as finished works of art, as were the frescoes.

These many contrasts between oil and fresco are evident in Brumidi's battle scenes for the lunettes in the Military Affairs Committee room. The oil sketches successfully convey the spontaneity of the conflict. We see and feel the action: smoke from the battle scene curling into the sky, blood spilling onto the ground, and the anguish of war etched into every soldier's face. The viewer's eyes are drawn to the central image, which is more detailed and complete than the figures at the edges of the composition. In contrast, in Brumidi's frescoes, all of the figures are consistently presented with the same level of detail in a more documentary manner. The sketches present a scene unfolding before the viewer, while the frescoes present a commemoration of an event.

In the oil sketch, *General Wooster at Ridgefield*, the garments of the dying general are rendered with gradations of strong colors that leap from the surface and create dramatic contrast and movement. In the fresco, the colors are softer and not as intense, making the fabric appear less dynamic. Such differences are also seen in *The Battle of Lexington*. The fresco presents a posed and controlled image of a British officer firing on the Minutemen from his rearing horse; the white steed looks statuesque. In contrast, in the sketch, the horse conveys utter terror, showing the white of his eye and what appears to be frothy blood in his mouth. With a few brushstrokes in oil, Brumidi conveys action, feeling, and movement. This intimate connection to the artist's creative process is the extra dimension the oil sketches provide.

Although Brumidi completed a total of six scenes for the Military Affairs Committee, he was unable to translate all of the preparatory images into frescoes, since Chairman Jefferson Davis of Mississippi wished to use the room. More than 10 years had elapsed when, in 1871, Senator Henry Wilson of Massachusetts, chairman of the committee during the Civil War, requested that the now-elderly Brumidi complete his work in the room. Brumidi proceeded to translate into fresco a scene from one of his earlier sketches, *Storming of Stony Point, General Wayne Wounded in the Head, Carried into the Fort*. The resulting fresco shows General "Mad Anthony" Wayne and his troops, victorious after a daring raid on the British garrison. Brumidi followed his preparatory study with very few compositional changes to the final fresco. He also created two new frescoes for the committee room, unrelated to the earlier preliminary sketches: *Washington at Valley Forge, 1778* and *The Boston Massacre, 1770*. Two of the six scenes from Brumidi's oil sketches were never completed for the room: *General Mercer's Death by Bayonet Stroke* and *The Americans at Sagg* [sic] *Harbor*

General Wooster at Ridgefield Mortally Wounded, Is Carried out of the Field (detail), oil on canvas sketch, ca. 1857.

The oil sketch shows fluid handling of the paint and lack of finish in the forms, qualities that lend a sense of immediacy to the scene. Oil sketches of this kind served the artist in developing the design and allowed examination and approval before the actual work on the fresco proceeded.

Death of General Wooster, 1777 (detail), fresco, **1858**.

Having conceptualized the overall composition in his preparatory sketch, Brumidi was able to refine the level of finish in the individual figures in his fresco. He included even the smallest element, such as the silhouetted figures emerging from the battle smoke, seen in the lower right corner.

Death of General Montgomery and The Battle of Lexington, oil on canvas sketch, ca. 1857.

The Battle of Lexington, fresco, 1858.

The Americans at Sagg [sic] *Harbor Burned Twelve Brigs and Sloops, and* [illegible] *Bringing with Him Many Prisoners* (detail), oil on canvas sketch, ca. 1857.

The oil medium allowed Brumidi to utilize contrasting colors to highlight key details. In his sketch of the Battle of Sag Harbor, he draws attention to the distant conflagration of the British ships, *far right*, not only by turning the figures towards the action, but also by boldly accenting the colonel's cloak, the American flag, and the torch flame held aloft.

Burned Twelve Brigs and Sloops, and [illegible] *Bringing with Him Many Prisoners*. A detail from the third sketch, *Death of General Montgomery*, was painted on the ceiling to resemble a carved stone relief. When completed, the room for the Senate Committee on Military Affairs and Militia was one of the most nationalist in theme in the Capitol. In a eulogy to Brumidi in 1880, Senator Daniel Voorhees of Indiana lavished praise on the artwork, asking: "Who ever passed through the room of the Committee on Military Affairs without feeling that the very genius of heroism had left there its immortal inspirations?" [11]

The final sketch by Brumidi in this collection served as a preparatory study for the Senate Reception Room, originally called "the antechamber of the Senate." The sketch depicts four allegorical figures: Liberty, Peace, Plenty, and War. Brumidi began his designs for the elaborate room even before completing his work in the House Committee on Agriculture. Meigs wrote in December 1855: "Brumidi brought me a design sketch in pencil for the decoration of the Senate anteroom. It is beautiful. He is full of innovation, and this, if worked up with skill, will make a beautiful room." [12]

Although Brumidi submitted his initial pencil sketch and a detailed design plan for the Senate Reception Room by early 1856, work on the room occurred sporadically over many years, with Brumidi modifying his designs for its murals in the process.[13] Around 1858, Brumidi prepared an oil sketch, *Liberty, Peace, Plenty, War*, for the room, but he did not paint the fresco on the Reception Room's vaulted ceiling until 1869. The sketch shows Brumidi's virtuosity at perspective and foreshortening. With just a few well-placed brush strokes, Brumidi creates the illusion of cherubs soaring through the air as they are engaged in their various activities. The most significant change from sketch to fresco is evidenced in the figure of Peace. In the oil sketch, Brumidi identifies Peace with

her attribute of a rainbow and an olive wreath. Peace reaches to set fire to a pile of weapons. In the fresco, however, Brumidi depicts a serene figure bearing an olive branch in one hand, and in the other, the tools of the arts: paintbrushes and an architect's triangle and compass. A nearby cherub offers a lyre and trumpet to Peace, while another cherub dramatically discards the symbols of war: a shield, helmet, and sword.

The five oil sketches once owned by the Macomb family are just a few of the more than 30 known preparatory sketches in oil, watercolor, or pencil that Brumidi executed for his Capitol murals.[14] They comprised the largest, still-intact private collection of Brumidi's preparatory studies for the building; the collection was a significant one, preserved for generations. The relationship between

Liberty, Peace, Plenty, War, **oil on canvas sketch, ca. 1858.**

Brumidi's sketch celebrates the nation's history, achievements, and symbols with depictions of eagles, a cornucopia, a plow, and a locomotive.

Opposite: **Senate Reception Room.**

This highly decorated room continues to serve its original purpose as a meeting place for senators and constituents.

Top: **Peace, detail from *Liberty, Peace, Plenty, War*, oil on canvas sketch, ca. 1858.**

Bottom: **Peace, detail from *Liberty, Peace, Plenty, War*, fresco, 1869.**

Brumidi dramatically altered the figure of Peace from his preparatory oil sketch to the fresco on the Senate Reception Room ceiling. In the interim, more than ten years had elapsed, and the Civil War had been fought.

Meigs and the Macomb family unquestionably played a role in the latter's acquisition of these historic sketches.

Meigs' work at the Capitol and his personal life were closely intertwined. In 1841, Meigs married Louisa Rodgers, the daughter of Minerva Denison Rodgers and Commodore John Rodgers, a venerated naval hero of the Barbary War; nine years later, Louisa's sister, Ann "Nannie" Rodgers, married John Navarre Macomb, Jr. The families quickly became attached, as evidenced by John and Nannie's naming their first child Montgomery Meigs Macomb. John served with the Army Department of Topographical Engineers and spent considerable time away from his family on various expeditions. During his absence, Nannie and the children lived with the Meigs family

Although the sketches may not have been considered fine art at the time, evidently both Brumidi and Meigs considered them worth saving.

in Washington, D.C., and Nannie wrote frequently to her husband about family matters, the Washington social scene, and Meigs' work at the Capitol.

Montgomery Meigs and John Macomb shared a close friendship and career interests. Both were engineers and army men. During Macomb's visits home, the gentlemen took long walks into the neighboring countryside, attended receptions with their wives, and reviewed the work at the Capitol. Macomb consoled Meigs when Meigs buried a stillborn daughter. When Meigs was called away to serve as quartermaster general during the early years of the Civil War, he placed Macomb in charge of the construction of the Capitol extension. Although the Meigs and Macomb families moved to different parts of the country after the war, the two men continued to correspond until Macomb passed away in 1889.

While records indicate that Brumidi saved most of his preparatory oil sketches, leaving them on his death to his son Laurence, apparently Meigs also retained some of the artist's sketches.[15] Although the sketches may not have been considered fine art at the time, evidently both Brumidi and Meigs considered them worth saving. After Meigs died in 1892, his Brumidi sketches came into the Macomb family's possession.

It is unknown exactly how the Macomb family acquired the five Brumidi sketches. In 1950, Myrtle Cheney Murdock, the wife of Congressman John Murdock of Arizona, wrote the first monograph on Brumidi: *Constantino Brumidi: Michelangelo of the Capitol.* She recorded that, after the death of Montgomery Meigs, some of Brumidi's "originals" were given to John Macomb's youngest son, Colonel Augustus Canfield Macomb (Meigs' nephew), although her source for this information was not provided and cannot be verified.[16] The Macomb family offered two alternatives regarding the provenance of the sketches. One possibility is that Colonel Augustus Macomb purchased the sketches from the estate sale of Montgomery Meigs in 1892. However, records from the estate sale do not list any Brumidi paintings. The second possibility is that Montgomery Meigs originally presented the sketches to Montgomery Meigs Macomb, since the young man had served as Meigs' aide-de-camp during the Civil War.

Despite ambiguity about how the Macomb family acquired the Brumidi oil sketches, the family, with its history of military service to the nation, highly esteemed its collection of Brumidi's works. Colonel Augustus Macomb "traveled from one army post to another over a quarter of a century . . . and always the beautiful Brumidi paintings went along."[17] According to the recollections of his son, Captain Alexander Macomb, the sketches hung in an adobe house at Fort Huachuca, Arizona, now known as Crook House. Colonel Augustus Macomb

John Navarre Macomb, Jr. (1811–1889).

Augustus Canfield Macomb (1854–1932), son of John N. Macomb, Jr.

lived there from July 1900 to March 1901, when he commanded Troop A, 5th Cavalry Regiment. Augustus Macomb later left the sketches to Alexander.

As the sketches descended through the Macomb family, a greater national appreciation for Constantino Brumidi and his work emerged, as research and restoration brought forward new information on the artist. The start of a comprehensive mural conservation program in 1981 under the Architect of the Capitol focused renewed attention on Brumidi's artistic contributions. As a result, the Macomb descendants recognized the significance of these early Brumidi sketches to the history of the Capitol and relinquished the care of this century-old collection to Congress with the sentiment, "The Brumidi sketches are now back where they belong."[18]

The sketches are a small and intimate chapter in the larger story of how the U.S. Capitol has come to be the magnificent and inspiring building it is today. It is the seat of government, a symbol of democracy, and a patriotic shrine for the nation. For over 200 years, countless figures, both public and private, have worked together to make the building and its art as stirring as the ideals they stand for. Brumidi's five oil sketches are now part of the Senate and House of Representatives collections, thanks to a collective patriotic endeavor: an army engineer who loved art as well as his country, an Italian-born artist who was inspired by the history of his adopted homeland, and a family steeped in military tradition who appreciated the historic significance of this artwork.

Constantino Brumidi's plantation desk, early 19th century.

Brumidi's desk is inscribed on the back "Brooklyn NY" and suggests a connection to the city where he first arrived and lived in this country.

Brumidi's Plantation Desk

On February 19, 1880, Constantino Brumidi died from kidney failure at his Washington, D.C., home. The funeral, held the next day at his three-story brick house, was attended by George F.W. Strieby, one of Brumidi's assistants and the person to whom Brumidi entrusted his mahogany plantation desk.

The drop-front mahogany desk was likely used at Brumidi's home studio, "a pleasant room given up to casts, pictures and music." [19] The studio is where Brumidi completed preliminary sketches for his murals, "so that all the work done at the Capitol [was] simply the mechanical execution." [20] A wall of the parlor studio was devoted to "half-finished designs" [21] and had a space the exact width of the Rotunda frieze marked off.[22] Confined at home because of ill health in the final days of his life, Brumidi was working on the "Battle of Lexington" cartoon for the Rotunda frieze.

The recipient of Brumidi's mahogany desk, George Strieby, was born in Bavaria and immigrated to the United States in 1853. He lived in Washington, D.C., with Emmerich A. Carstens, foreman of the decorative painters for the Capitol extension. Strieby served as an apprentice and then decorative painter at the Capitol for five years and worked closely with Brumidi from 1877 to 1879. When Strieby died in 1908, the desk descended to his son, Philip, also a decorative painter, and then to his granddaughter, Anna Strieby Fogle, who donated the desk to the Senate in 1971.

Conserved maiden panel (detail), Senate Appropriations Committee Room.

Conservation restored the graceful, floating quality of the nine maidens featured on the room's wall panels.

Continuing Conservation of Brumidi's Murals in the U.S. Capitol

Barbara A. Wolanin

Freed from dark and clumsy overpaint, many of Constantino Brumidi's original murals can now be seen and understood in ways that have not been possible for more than a century. Restoration began in the early 1980s, when the Architect of the Capitol launched a long-term mural conservation program sparked by the burgeoning fields of historic preservation and professional fine art conservation.[1] The accomplishments of the first decade of the conservation program are highlighted in the 1998 publication *Constantino Brumidi: Artist of the Capitol.*[2] Since then, numerous conservation studies and treatments have revealed more about the beauty and sophistication of the Capitol's 19th-century murals.

Trained in Rome, Brumidi arrived in America a master in painting life-like classical figures and forms that appear to be three dimensional, or trompe l'oeil. He was a brilliant colorist, skilled in a variety of paint mediums, including true fresco. Brumidi carried out the vision of Montgomery C. Meigs, supervising engineer of the Capitol extension, for a Capitol with walls and ceilings filled with murals in the Renaissance tradition. Within two decades of Brumidi's death, however, inferior artists and decorative painters began to touch up and completely repaint his murals with oil-based paint, unfortunately matching their colors to grime, previous overpaint, or yellowed varnish.

Brumidi's First Room, H–144

Brumidi created his first Capitol mural in the new House wing, in the room designated for the House Agriculture Committee. He successfully demonstrated his skill in painting in true fresco, which must be painted on sections of fresh plaster applied each day and which allows the pigments to become part of the wall as the plaster cures. According to Meigs, this was the first time fresco had been used in this country. Meigs brought many prominent figures to view Brumidi's work in progress, including President Franklin Pierce, Secretary of War Jefferson Davis, and art collector William Corcoran. Meigs put Brumidi on the payroll and directed him to fill the room with murals, and the artist finished the room's lunettes, walls, and ceiling in 1856. Brumidi's convincing trompe l'oeil effects made the room a popular attraction for visitors.[3]

A small fire in the committee room in 1920, as well as soot from years of fireplace use, led to more than one repainting of the room's lunettes and wall murals in darker colors. When the figurative murals on the ceiling and lunettes were conserved in 1987 and 1988, testing showed that the walls below the lunettes had been originally painted in true fresco to look like stone with arched moldings. This illusionistic effect was obscured by the overpaint, and in 2005, the walls were fully restored. After removing multiple layers of oil paint, conservators reduced the unsightly appearance of soot-filled cracks on the original fresco and skillfully inpainted damaged areas to match the original color and surface appearance.[4] Now, 150 years after Brumidi painted his first room in the Capitol, one can appreciate his sophisticated murals, which create a Renaissance-inspired illusion of a room constructed

Architect of the Capitol

House Agriculture Committee Room after conservation of the murals on the ceiling, lunettes, and walls.

The walls, the only ones in the Capitol that Brumidi painted in true fresco, show his skill in executing trompe l'oeil moldings that resemble carved stone arches.

of stone with vaults open to a blue sky in which deities representing the four seasons float on clouds.

The Senate Appropriations Committee Room, S–127

As Brumidi was completing his first room, Meigs had the artist turn his attention to designs for the new Senate wing, which was still under construction. The room planned for the Naval Affairs Committee was decorated by Brumidi with images related to the sea and sailing. The room was later assigned to the Senate Committee on Appropriations, which continues to occupy this beautifully decorated space. The murals were inspired by first-century Roman wall paintings from "the precious monuments of Pompeii and the baths of Titus."[5] Brumidi's watercolor design for the committee room offered two different color schemes. The option with the blue background found in some Roman murals, more suitable for naval and marine themes, was selected rather than the more typical "Pompeian red" background. Images of classical gods and goddesses, such as Neptune and Venus, as well as sea creatures, are interspersed throughout the ceiling.

Design for the Naval Affairs Committee Room, watercolor, 1856.

This watercolor sketch, approved and signed by Meigs on August 20, 1856, shows the Pompeian-style designs proposed by Brumidi for the room's ceiling and wall murals.

On the brilliant blue panels on the lower walls, Brumidi painted maidens who hold objects related to the sea and sailing and seem to float gracefully in the air. The panels are framed by trompe l'oeil pilasters and ledges supporting cornucopias of flowers. Above the doors, he placed pairs of genii (winged cherubs with acanthus leaves forming the lower halves of their bodies) holding the striped shield of the United States, set against striking black backgrounds.[6]

Over the years, soot and grime from the fireplace, open windows, and tobacco smoke, as well as yellowed varnish, discolored the blue fields, or backgrounds, so much that they were repainted a heavy dark green, imprisoning the maidens so that they no longer seemed to float. In 1978, shortly before the Architect of the Capitol mural conservation program began, in-house decorative painters "restored" the room by reworking damaged areas, repainting the panels in an even darker green, and brushing a yellowing varnish over all of the walls. Fortunately, on the ceiling, the plain fields were repainted in colors very close to the original, and Brumidi's true fresco figures were left largely untouched.

Conservation in the Senate Appropriations Committee Room began in 2003 with scientific testing and analysis to understand the materials and the conditions of the murals.[7] Recovering the true color of the maiden panels

Senate Appropriations Committee Room before and after conservation.

Before conservation, *left*, overpaint and yellowed varnish obscured details in the wall and lunette murals. The restored murals, *right*, can now be appreciated with their original brilliant colors and three-dimensional forms.

was a priority. Brumidi's 1856 watercolor sketch, early photographs, small exposure windows made by conservators, and a cleaned area on the panel behind the room's gilded mirror all verified the original color. In 2005, the panels were fully conserved, and layers of green overpaint were removed to reveal Brumidi's vibrant blue. Cleaned of yellowed varnish and overpaint, the trompe l'oeil frames surrounding the panels could once again be appreciated.

Testing of area behind mirror, Senate Appropriations Committee Room.

Conservators first revealed the original blue field in this area located behind the room's large gilded mirror.

Maiden panel (detail), Senate Appropriations Committee Room.

This photograph shows the striking contrast between the original brilliant blue of the backgrounds and the dark green overpaint.

Partially restored panel of genii with American shield, Senate Appropriations Committee Room.

The delicate, rich colors and three-dimensional quality of the genius on the left were revealed after the removal of yellowed varnish.

Damaged maiden panel during and after conservation, Senate Appropriations Committee Room.

The most severely damaged of the maiden panels is shown with paint losses after the removal of heavy overpaint, *left*, and after the missing areas of the blue field were carefully recreated, *right*.

Cornucopia with flowers before and after conservation, Senate Appropriations Committee Room.

The overpainted cornucopia, *left*, had been given a heavier arrangement of roses and leaves. The restored original mural, *right*, features morning glories and delicate tendrils.

The panels' graceful maidens in their iridescent dresses were brought back to life, and incredibly delicate details were recovered, such as the line on one maiden's fishing pole. Some of the cornucopias of dainty flowers on the illusionistic ledge had been significantly altered, changing the colors and the types of flowers. Other cornucopias were found to be badly damaged under the overpaint and had to be sensitively recreated based on those on other walls that had remained intact under the overpaint.

Conservation of the lunettes above the maiden panels was another challenge that ultimately helped confirm the written history about the painting of the committee room's lunettes. Camillo Bisco, an artist hired to help Brumidi, painted the committee room's lunettes with the Pompeian architectural perspectives suggested in Brumidi's watercolor sketch. Each of the six architectural perspectives contains a central area that was intended to be filled with a naval battle scene. Bisco, however, was fired in early 1858, after completing only one lunette in its entirety. In 1978, the central areas were repainted with fields of a jarring, flat light gray.

Conservators consolidated detached paint in the lunettes so that they could safely clean the murals of grime and overpaint. They found that water leaks had destroyed much of Bisco's painting in his one completed lunette, leaving the design compromised and eliminating the option of replicating Bisco's scene in the other lunettes' central areas. Instead, the solution for the blank areas was to remove overpaint and recreate the shadowy neutral tone, leaving them as they looked in Brumidi's lifetime.

Left: **Exposure windows in the northwest lunette, Senate Appropriations Committee Room.**

The overpainted lunette was tested to explore underlying layers of paint.

Below: **Conserved northwest lunette, Senate Appropriations Committee Room.**

Beneath overpaint in the northwest lunette, conservators found the central area's shadowy neutral color. This effect was replicated in the remaining lunettes.

Architect of the Capitol

Treating lifting tempera paint in the lunettes, Senate Appropriations Committee Room.

Before cleaning and overpaint removal could begin, conservators consolidated lifting paint.

Architect of the Capitol

Evidence of mural painted by one of Brumidi's assistants, Senate Appropriations Committee Room.

The artist's signature, "G. West," was found inscribed in the plaster with "Delt.," an abbreviation for "Delineator."

In addition, the lunettes were tested to determine if anything remained of six earlier paintings of War of 1812 naval battles. These battle scenes are documented in Meigs' journal and correspondence, although no photographs or sketches of the paintings are known. The scenes were painted in 1856 by George West, a young American painter whom Meigs had hired to work under Brumidi. Although West complained that he deserved higher pay, Meigs was not happy with his work. Since Meigs had refused West's angry offer to erase his scenes, the possibility remained that they might still be recoverable beneath the overpaint. However, testing found only small fragments of color, showing that West's paintings had indeed been scraped off and are now lost to history. Conservators did discover that West had pressed so hard in signing his name that it remains inscribed in the plaster, tangible confirmation that he had worked in the room.

In 2010 and 2011, conservators removed discolored varnish and selective overpaint on the rest of the committee room's lower walls above the faux marbleized dado and uncovered the brilliance of the colors. The conservators also restored the full three-dimensional effect that Brumidi had created in the figures and marbleized pilasters.[8] Since the murals on the ceiling vaults remain close to their original appearance, they are a lower priority for conservation but will be addressed in the future.

**Portrait of a Child with Moth,
oil on canvas, 1853.**

Brumidi combined portraiture
with allegory in this representation
of Kate Bennitt.

U.S. Senate Collection

Portrait of a Child with Moth

In 1852, Constantino Brumidi immigrated to America and resided
briefly in New York City. To establish himself as an artist during
these initial years in America, he accepted commissions such as
Portrait of a Child with Moth. An inscription on the reverse of this
painting identifies the young sitter as Kate Bennitt.

Brumidi's portrait of Kate is similar in style to three allegorical
scenes, *Hope*, *Plenty*, and *Progress*, that Brumidi executed for a ceiling in the Bennitt family's home in Southampton, Long Island. Two
of the paintings depict female figures adorned with billowing drapery
and set against a background of clouds. In *Child with Moth*, Brumidi
places two-and-a-half-year-old Kate in a setting of heavenly clouds.
She wears a pink silk drape rather than contemporary Victorian
attire, and her hands delicately cradle a large moth.

In painting and literature, butterflies and moths traditionally
represent transience. Victorians viewed childhood as an idealistic
phase of life with a distinct identity of its own. The moth serves
as an attribute of childhood, representing the delicate nature of
youth and the fleeting passage of time. This sense of fragility and
the impending darkness of the clouds in *Child with Moth* are all the
more poignant with hindsight: Kate would not survive her eighth
birthday. Child mortality rates were high in the 19th century, and
parents often lost more than one offspring to childhood illnesses.
Catherine Eulalie Bennitt (Kate), born on October 7, 1851, died
October 5, 1859, just shy of her birthday. A brother died in infancy.

Washington with Jefferson and Hamilton, painted by Brumidi in 1872, flanked by portraits of 20th-century senators, Senate Reception Room.

Two blank rondels were filled in 2004 with portraits of Senators Arthur H. Vandenberg, *left*, and Robert F. Wagner, *right*.

The Senate Reception Room, S–213

The Senate Reception Room, located near the Senate chamber, is one of the most highly ornamented rooms in the Capitol. Like many of the other spaces Brumidi decorated, the Reception Room has undergone extensive conservation in recent years. Restoring the complex decorative scheme has taken years of study and work by experienced conservators, as well as the ongoing support and commitment of the Architect of the Capitol, Senate leadership, and Congress.

Brumidi submitted a first sketch and written proposal for the allegorical subjects on the Senate Reception Room ceiling in 1855. During the next two decades, Brumidi added murals to the room, although he never completed all of the portraits that he planned for the impressive and richly decorated space. The room's intricate gilded cast plaster decorations, consisting of plant forms and classical motifs punctuated by eagles and stags, were created by head ornamental plasterer Ernest Thomas and gilded by François Hugot. The lower walls were finished with scagliola (imitation marble) in several colors. By 1858, Brumidi had painted the cherubs in the center of the ceiling's dome, and for the pendentives, completed allegorical figures of the four cardinal virtues: Prudence, Justice, Fortitude, and Temperance. Once construction of the Capitol extension was completed, murals could no longer be paid for with construction funds, and Brumidi was removed from the payroll. Commissions for him to add murals were sporadic. Not until 1869 was he hired to paint the scenes of Liberty, Peace, Plenty, and War in the groin vaults on the north end of the Senate Reception Room. In 1870 and 1871, Brumidi designed and painted trompe l'oeil figures of maidens and cherubs to resemble marble sculpture in the lunettes. Finally, in 1872, he was paid to fill one of the blank areas on the south lunette with a scene of President Washington, Thomas Jefferson, and Alexander Hamilton. His 1876 petition to fill the remaining spaces in the room with portraits of presidents was unsuccessful. A century after Brumidi had proposed portraits of "illustrious men" for the ovals on the walls, the Senate made the decision to fill the ovals with five portraits of notable senators. These portraits were painted on canvas and installed in 1959. Three of the rondels that Brumidi left blank were filled in 2004 and 2006 with portraits of 20th-century senators and a double portrait depicting the authors of the Connecticut Compromise.[9]

Opposite: **Pilot treatment on the west wall, Senate Reception Room.**

The pilot area included one of every kind of panel: the portrait panel on the left; the central pilaster's putti panel, Greek key border, and flanking candelabra panels; and the disc panel on the right.

Brumidi's murals in the Senate Reception Room have been subject to damage from repairs following an explosion, discoloration from layers of grime and tobacco smoke, and extensive and misguided overpaint. A full repainting and clumsy overgilding were carried out throughout the room in 1930. Conservation of the Senate Reception Room began in the mid-1990s with Brumidi's figurative frescoes and murals.[10] Attention later turned to restoring the ornate gilded cast plaster and decorative painting that are such an important part of the aesthetic plan. Decisions about how to restore each of the dozens of painted or gilded decorative elements were guided by an intensive study, which included microscopic analysis of scores of tiny extracted samples and the creation of numerous exposures of the original color and finish by careful removal of later layers. The analysis verified that the original decorative paint finishes were composed of thin layers and glazes that softened and enriched the final appearance. The shiny, burnished water gilding—applied in 1857 to highlight features of the cast plaster leaves, flowers, ears of corn, sheaves of wheat, and classical

decoration—was discovered largely intact and recoverable under layers of dark brown overpaint and overgilding. However, the original matte oil gilding on most of the plaster moldings could not be separated from the oil overpaint, and these elements had to be skillfully regilded.

A pilot treatment of the Senate Reception Room's west wall included testing on the three types of wall panels that repeat throughout the room. Because of the complexity of the decoration, restoration was carried out by professional gilding and painting conservators working alongside skilled decorative painters, all interacting with the curators during the analysis and decision-making process. Dark brown overpaint was painstakingly removed from the borders of one of the pilot panels. Conservators identified the borders' original pinkish-tan color resembling sandstone, and these original surfaces exposed by conservators served as the model for the replication of other borders.[11] Exposures on the painted areas surrounding the shimmering gold botanical forms and classical moldings revealed delicate tones of warm light stone, coppery brown, and soft green. These colors were carefully replicated on other

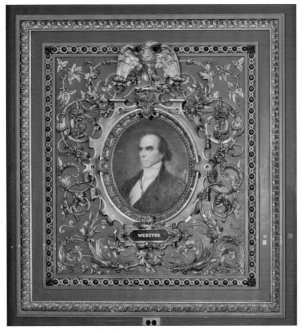
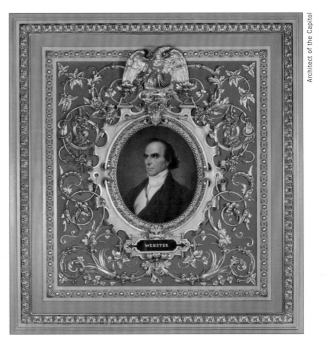

Webster portrait panel before and after conservation, Senate Reception Room.

Before restoration, layers of dark overpaint and inappropriate gilding gave the panel a drab appearance, *left*. Restoration of the original paint colors and brilliant gilding brought out the sophisticated, dynamic quality of the plaster ornamentation, *right*.

panels, as were the stone-like borders and the trompe l'oeil Greek key patterns simulating carved stone.

At the same time, conservators worked on sections of the room's lunettes. They consolidated detached plaster, removed jarring overpaint, and softened the appearance of the blank areas that Brumidi had intended to fill with portraits of presidents.[12]

With the pilot treatment completed, the sophisticated palette and decorative scheme that Brumidi and his assistants created became evident. The sections restored in the pilot area not only illustrate how the original wall decorations complemented Brumidi's figurative frescoes and murals, but also set the standard for the restoration of the decorative wall panels in the rest of the room.

Architect of the Capitol

Conservator regilding cast plaster ornaments, Senate Reception Room.

This intricate work requires skill and patience, as well as a thorough understanding of the historic gilding patterns.

Architect of the Capitol

Architect of the Capitol

Pilot treatment of stone-colored borders, Senate Reception Room.

The original Greek key pattern in light colors resembling stone was completely covered by dark brown overpaint. (The candelabra panel's borders and cast-plaster gilded moldings are shown already restored.)

Replicating the Greek key design, Senate Reception Room.

Conservation of the pilot panels helped determine the best methods for restoring the walls in the room. Here, the decorative painter replicates the trompe l'oeil Greek key design.

The Brumidi Corridors

The restoration of the Brumidi Corridors has been the most large-scale mural conservation project in the Capitol, in terms of the extent of Brumidi's work that has been uncovered and the time that has been devoted to the restoration. The impressive vaulted Brumidi Corridors crisscross the first floor of the Senate wing, and the conservation project has brought about dramatic changes to the appearance of the murals designed, and in part painted, by Brumidi himself. The murals on the walls and pilasters are divided into panels framed by trompe l'oeil molding and filled with complex decorative motifs. No two panels are identical, making them worthy of fine art conservation rather than treatment as decorative painting with uniformly repeated patterns. For more than a century, Brumidi's murals, which were easily damaged because of their location in busy passageways, were retouched or repainted in ever-darkening colors by artists or decorative painters at a time when repainting was the commonly accepted way to restore them.

Over the years, discoveries resulting from research have added to the understanding of the corridors' designs and subjects. For example, one scholar was able to locate in the New York Public Library the oversized volumes with hand-colored plates of Raphael's loggia that had inspired Meigs when he saw them at the Astor Library. Meigs noted in his journal, "They have 3 volumes—the pilasters, the arabesque[s], and the loggias. I have never seen colored engraving of these works before. They are very beautiful, rich and harmonious in color, simple and beautiful in design. I wish I could see the rooms themselves. This book will give us ideas in decorating our lobbies." [13] Also, studies of the birds, butterflies, and flowers in the conserved wall panels have increased appreciation of the way in which American flora and fauna are accurately documented in the Capitol's murals. [14] In addition, paint analysis and testing, as well as the opening of exposure windows throughout the corridors, have provided more understanding of the original appearance and materials of the 19th-century murals and wall decoration, such as the trompe l'oeil inlaid and carved stone designs discovered during recent testing, which will serve to guide future restoration. [15]

Conservation in the Brumidi Corridors started in 1985 with the lunettes over committee room doors. These historical scenes and portraits were painted by Brumidi himself in true fresco. Once the lunettes were conserved, attention turned to the wall murals below the cornice. Recovery of the elaborately decorated original panels hidden under muddy green and dirty

Right: **Engraving by Giovanni Ottaviani of a panel from Raphael's loggia (detail), in** *Loggie de Rafaele nel Vaticano,* **ca. 1772–77.**

Far right: **Panel with chipmunks (detail), Brumidi Corridors (North Corridor).**

Hand-colored engravings from a book on Raphael's loggia, *right,* impressed Meigs and provided ideas for the designs in the Senate's corridors, *far right.*

New York Public Library

Architect of the Capitol

yellow overpaint began in 1996. A successful pilot project was carried out in the Patent Corridor, where Brumidi painted portraits of inventors in the lunettes. It proved that Brumidi's original designs and colors in the panels and trompe l'oeil borders were in remarkably good condition under the layers of overpaint and could be recovered. Replication was necessary only for the plain stone-colored borders and was guided by exposure windows that revealed the original color. Surprisingly, as the work progressed over the next decade, subtle variations were discovered in the colors of the repeating elements, such as the stone-colored borders, molded cornices, and star bands over doorways. These differences may have been intentional, to suggest different light sources, or could have resulted from the use of hand-mixed colors by different painters working under varied lighting conditions.

Following the conservation of the wall murals in the Patent Corridor, the restoration proceeded through the long North Corridor. This hallway is painted with elaborately decorated panels featuring pairs of birds, arrangements of fruits and flowers, and illusionistic relief profile portraits of Revolutionary-era leaders, as

Panel with illusionistic relief portrait of Revolutionary War General Richard Montgomery, Brumidi Corridors (North Corridor).

A comparison of the panels before conservation, *left*, and after conservation, *right*, shows how the subtle colors, details, and three-dimensional effects were lost during repainting over the years.

well as panels depicting trophies of symbolic objects. Recovery of Brumidi's original designs continued down the West Corridor, with its illusionistic relief portraits of signers of the Declaration of Independence and diminutive classical gods and goddesses.[16]

As conservation of the walls progressed for more than a decade, it was discovered that the condition of the panels varied greatly. Plaster failing from loss of cohesion or detachment from the brick wall was found to some extent on most of the panels. The conservators gradually refined materials and techniques for strengthening the plaster. A system of hanging bottles and tubes resembling a medical IV drip allowed a consolidant fluid to flow gently and effectively into the voids and unstable areas. Once the plaster was treated,

conservators could painstakingly remove the layers of oil overpaint. Any lost details were carefully inpainted. Panel by panel, Brumidi's original designs in the vivid shades of red, white, and blue described in early guide books were brought back to view. Many surprising and beautiful details were recovered, such as a little ear of corn, the expressive face of a squirrel, or the graceful form of a classical deity. To illustrate how discolored the walls were prior to conservation, a section of an overpainted panel has been left in the east stairwell.

One of the greatest challenges for the conservators of the Brumidi Corridors was the North Entry. Although the North Entry's original tempera ceiling murals remained intact, early testing on the overpainted walls was inconclusive, and the original murals were not found

Left: **Wall panel during conservation testing, Brumidi Corridors (West Corridor).**

The soft white fields and fresh colors of the original 1850s designs slowly came back into view as conservators removed overpaint and yellowed varnish.

Below: **Conservator at work, Brumidi Corridors.**

After removing layers of overpaint, the conservator carefully applies reversible materials to areas where the original paint is missing.

at that time. Aided by years of experience in the rest of the corridors, conservators were finally able to uncover original designs buried under a heavy green paint. Two panels in the North Entry had been replastered long ago and did not contain any original design. They were replicated based on neighboring panels, and this replication helped restore the symmetry of the space.[17]

The Zodiac Corridor

The north section of the West Corridor got its name from the signs of the zodiac on brilliant blue fields that Brumidi painted above the cornice on the highly decorated, barrel-vaulted ceiling. The wide panels on the walls are painted similarly to those in the adjoining corridors, which feature trophies of symbolic objects

Ceiling before and after restoration, Brumidi Corridors (Zodiac Corridor).

Overpaint compromised the sophisticated design and dramatically altered the colors, *above left*. After conservation, *left*, the ceiling's murals once again resembled gathered fabric panels.

attributed to the English artist James Leslie and illusionistic relief portraits painted by Brumidi. Like the rest of the Brumidi Corridors, the original murals on the walls and ceiling of the Zodiac Corridor were hidden under layers of overpaint. The ceiling, originally painted in tempera, had also been periodically damaged by water leaks from pipes above, necessitating repairs and repainting numerous times. In the early 1980s, the signs of the zodiac were repainted with different and larger designs.

Conservation of Pisces, Brumidi Corridors (Zodiac Corridor).

The large overpainted zodiac sign concealed Brumidi's original, smaller sign. The bottom fish, partially conserved, shows the size difference between the original and the overpainted fish.

Panel with trophies and flowers during and after the conservation process, Brumidi Corridors (Zodiac Corridor).

As conservation progressed, *left*, the refinement of the original wall murals became apparent, *right*.

Opposite: **Restored ceiling and wall murals, Brumidi Corridors (Zodiac Corridor).**

Conservation of the area began in 2012. Unstable plaster and paint were consolidated, and to the extent possible, overpaint was removed from the ceiling. This work revealed the colors and designs of the tempera ceiling, transforming the fields from dirty yellow to creamy white and bringing back the jewel-like tones of the original. Where Brumidi's designs had been washed away by water leaks, they were reconstructed from similar images on the opposite side of the ceiling vault. Where heavy applications of oil overpaint could not be removed, the correct colors were replicated based on the original colors identified by the conservators.

Cleaning the wall panels revealed the delicate details of the trophies and flowers. The panel with a portrait of Robert Morris (a financier of the American Revolution) was discovered to be a reproduction on new plaster that closely followed the design on the opposite wall. Since the original panel no longer existed, the reproduction panel was toned to better harmonize with the colors and style of the adjacent original panels. At the end of the project, a wall that for 10 years had separated the Zodiac Corridor from the West Corridor was removed.[18] Its removal reestablished the Zodiac Corridor as part of the Brumidi Corridors, returning the hallways to their original 19th century plan.[19]

Architect of the Capitol

Ceiling mural before and during conservation, Brumidi Corridors (Zodiac Corridor).

The fragile nature of tempera paint made the ceiling susceptible to water leaks that started to wash away the paint layer, *above left*. The same detail is shown during conservation, *left*.

The Trophy Room

With the goal of full restoration of the Brumidi Corridors, conservation priority shifted in 2011 to the area called the Trophy Room, which takes its name from the lunette murals that depict trophies of weapons and armor. Despite past treatment, lifting and flaking paint endangered the original ceiling mural. The first conservation challenge was to find materials that would readhere the lifting paint without darkening the colors. As with the other ceilings in the Brumidi Corridors, the Trophy Room's original illusionistic carved stone designs were painted in the water-based tempera medium. The ceiling vaults were found to have been crudely touched up in tempera at least two times; unfortunately, the similar composition of all the different paint layers made it impossible to remove the overpaint without taking the original paint along with it. The conservators therefore identified places where

Top: **Restored Trophy Room, Brumidi Corridors.**

Guided by evidence of the original mural, conservators restored the ceiling primarily by replication in this section of the Brumidi Corridors.

Bottom: **Flaking paint in the ceiling mural of the Trophy Room, Brumidi Corridors.**

Extreme flaking of multiple layers of delicate and porous tempera presented a challenge to the conservators.

Eagle and wreath before and after restoration, Trophy Room, Brumidi Corridors.

During the restoration process, the overpainted mural of an eagle and wreath, *left*, was carefully retouched, *right*, using evidence of the original colors to restore the mural's illusion of carved stone.

original colors were still visible and then retouched the overpainted designs to match, restoring the subtle effect of carved stone and moldings.[20] Due to extensive damage, the walls in the Trophy Room and the adjacent refectory area had to be replicated. While the condition of the Trophy Room did not allow for full recovery of the original decoration, the combination of restoration and replication has reestablished the quiet beauty of this room with illusionistic stone carvings.

Conservation of Brumidi's murals is methodical, painstaking work. Professional fine art conservation is far more involved than simply repainting the murals, as was the practice throughout most of the 20th

century. Today, many who visit the Capitol marvel at the fact that Brumidi worked in the building over a 25-year period. The mural conservation program at the Capitol has already taken longer than that and will continue for years to come. To date, much has been accomplished in the conservation of the Capitol's extensive murals. Detailed reports prepared by the conservators document methods, materials, and results for each project. This information will be invaluable for future treatment and maintenance so that Brumidi's unique Capitol murals are kept in good condition for the enjoyment and inspiration of future generations.

The Congressional Gold Medal was posthumously awarded to Brumidi in 2012, in recognition of his artistic contribution to the Capitol and the nation.

The Constantino Brumidi Congressional Gold Medal

On July 26, 2005, the 200th anniversary of his birth, Constantino Brumidi was honored by Congress with a joint ceremony in the Capitol Rotunda held under his masterpieces, *The Apotheosis of Washington* and the *Frieze of American History*. That year also marked the 150th anniversary of Brumidi's first fresco in the Capitol and the 125th anniversary of his death in 1880. Three years later, in 2008, Congress recognized Brumidi by authorizing a Congressional Gold Medal, one of the highest civilian awards in the United States.[21]

Congress has long presented gold medals to individuals who have performed outstanding deeds or acts of service to the security, prosperity, and national interest of the country; the first gold medal was awarded in 1776 to General George Washington. In recent years, the scope of the Congressional Gold Medal has expanded to include artists, writers, actors, scientists, explorers, athletes, and humanitarians, in addition to political and military leaders.

The front of Brumidi's gold medal bears an image of the artist based on a photograph taken by Montgomery C. Meigs. Depicted on the reverse is the central section of *The Apotheosis of Washington*. The medal was presented on July 11, 2012. Because there are no known descendants of Brumidi, the legislation authorized the medal to be displayed in the Capitol Visitor Center's Exhibition Hall, where it is seen by the millions of people each year who view Brumidi's murals on their tours of the U.S. Capitol.

Appendices

APPENDIX A—FLOOR PLAN OF THE BRUMIDI CORRIDORS, SENATE WING, U.S. CAPITOL

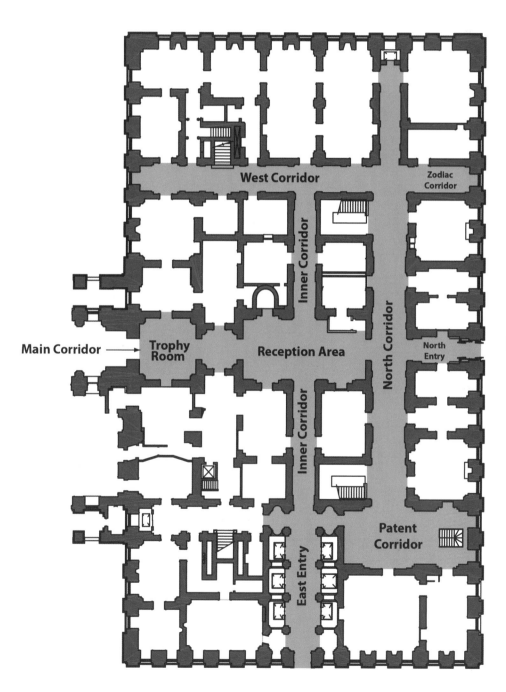

West Corridor

Zodiac Corridor

Inner Corridor

Main Corridor →

Trophy Room

Reception Area

North Corridor

North Entry

Inner Corridor

Patent Corridor

East Entry

Opposite: **Bronze railing (detail), designed by Brumidi and sculpted by Edmond Baudin, Brumidi Corridors (East Stairway), 1858–59.**

Appendix B—Map of the Pacific Railroad Survey Routes Indicating Locations Depicted in Constantino Brumidi's Landscape Medallions

Constantino Brumidi modeled eight landscape medallions in the Brumidi Corridors after illustrations in the 12-volume *Pacific Railroad Report*. The potential routes surveyed in 1853–54 for the first transcontinental railroad are noted in red; the numbered locations correspond to Brumidi's medallions (opposite page).

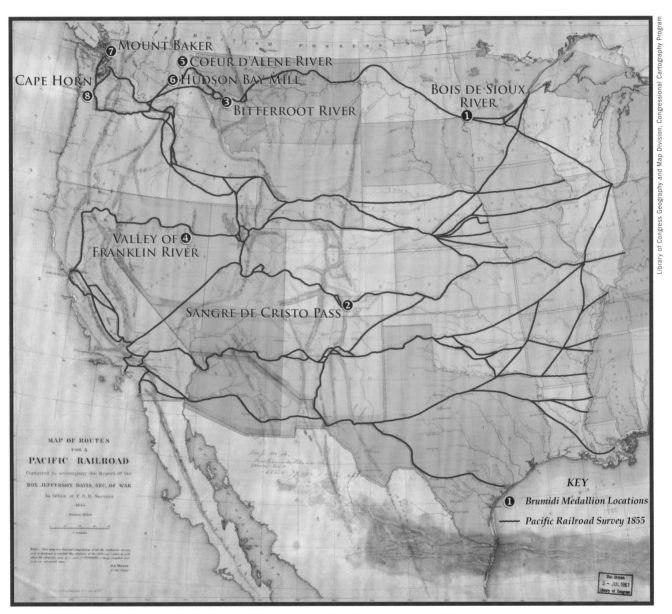

Adapted from G.K. Warren's 1855 *Map of Routes for a Pacific Railroad* (for original map, see page 59).

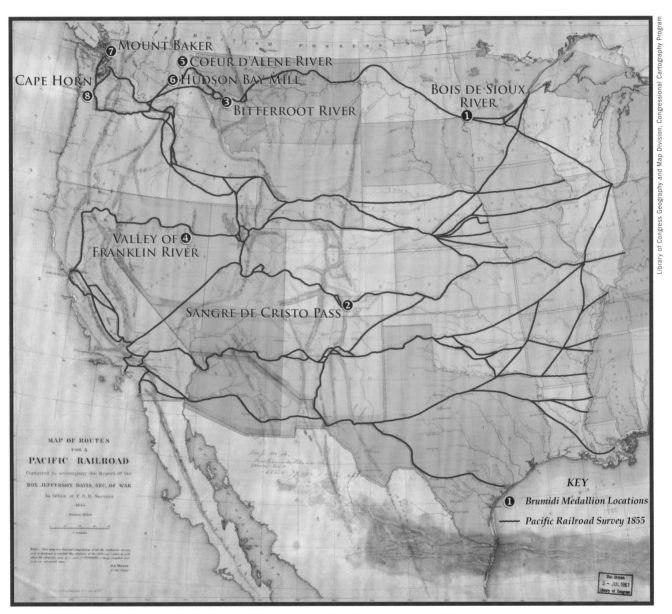

Bois de Sioux River (Minnesota)

Sangre de Cristo Pass (Colorado)

Bitterroot River (Montana)

Valley of Franklin River (Nevada)

Coeur d'Alene River (Idaho)

Hudson Bay Mill (Washington)

Mount Baker (Washington)

Cape Horn (Washington)

Architect of the Capitol

Acknowledgments

This project owes its existence to the leadership and support of Secretary of the Senate Nancy Erickson. Her commitment to the preservation of the historic spaces, furnishings, and art in the Senate wing of the Capitol reflects her sincere regard for the Senate as an institution. Senate Curator Diane K. Skvarla provided the impetus for this book and guided the effort with thoughtful advice every step of the way.

A publication like this relies upon the contributions of many people, especially the distinguished authors of chapters in this book, each of whom brought unique expertise and perspective to the project. I wish to thank a number of historians, curators, and professionals across a variety of fields who lent their time and knowledge. Smithsonian Institution specialists helped identify the species of birds and insects in Brumidi's murals: Curator of Birds Gary R. Graves, Curator of Lepidoptera Robert K. Robbins, and Curator of Natural History Rare Books Leslie Overstreet. Cartographer Jacqueline V. Nolan of the Library of Congress Congressional Cartography Program produced the Appendix B map that pinpoints geographic locations depicted in Brumidi's landscape medallions. Conservators Laurie Timm, Christy Cunningham-Adams, Bill Lewin, and Davida Kovner explained procedures and offered images to bring their specialized field to life in these pages.

In reviewing the manuscript, Architect of the Capitol Curator Barbara A. Wolanin shared her expertise on Brumidi's life and work, as well as her knowledge gained from managing the conservation of Brumidi's murals at the U.S. Capitol. Architectural Historian of the Capitol Emeritus William C. Allen generously provided review and valuable advice. Heartfelt thanks also go to the historians and art historians from outside the Senate who so kindly helped review and refine the manuscript, including Patricia LaBounty, Union Pacific Railroad Museum; Aileen Laing, Sweet Briar College; Charles V. Mutschler, Eastern Western University; Dave Shackelford, Baltimore and Ohio Railroad Museum; Gray Sweeny, Arizona State University; and Glenn Willumson, University of Florida. Bruce Burton, U.S. Department of State, provided critical insight and solved unique challenges that arose during the process of compiling this publication.

The staff of the Office of Senate Curator gave much appreciated support throughout the endeavor. Associate Curator Melinda Smith, Administrator Scott Strong, and Registrar Courtney Morfeld contributed to some of the shorter pieces in the book. Historic Preservation Officer Kelly Steele and Museum Specialist Richard Doerner took on fact-checking and caption writing. Collections Specialist Theresa Malanum orchestrated photography of Senate collection objects, particularly of Brumidi's oil on canvas sketches. She and Mr. Doerner also helped prepare several of the Capitol's rooms for photo shoots, while Executive Assistant Bryant Stukes and Collections Manager Deborah Wood helped review proofs as needed. Two student interns, Meredith Mitchell and Anna DiSilvestro, assisted with research. I am grateful for the help provided by each dedicated member of the Senate Curator's Office.

Additional colleagues in the Office of the Secretary of the Senate enhanced the character of the publication. From the Senate Historical Office, Historian Don Ritchie, Associate Historian Betty Koed, and Historical Editor Beth Hahn bestowed their knowledge and advice. Dot Svendson with the Executive Office lent her artistic eye. Staff members of the Senate Library, under the guidance of Senate Librarian Leona Faust, provided invaluable services. Nancy Kervin, reference librarian, accepted each research challenge with an adventurer's sense of discovery, and her colleague Brian McLaughlin supported the project in ways too many to list. The Secretary's Information Systems Office provided swift and helpful technical support during the process of creating the book.

This publication was a group effort that reached across many divisions, thanks to the staff of the Senate Sergeant at Arms Terrance W. Gainer and the Architect of the Capitol Stephen T. Ayers. A debt of gratitude is owed to Hilarie Gaylin, Senate Office of Education and Training, who undertook the task of editing over and above her many other responsibilities. Ms. Gaylin helped bring order and consistency to writings by multiple authors. I thank her for her expert and generous assistance.

To help illustrate this publication, Avon Ashton with the Senate Sergeant at Arms Office of Printing, Graphics, and Direct Mail managed the technical challenges of digitizing fragile, historic books that are works of art in their own right. Becky Daugherty, Senate Sergeant at Arms protocol officer, supported our frequent requests for permission to photograph the Capitol's interiors. Eric Paff with the Architect of the Capitol Curator's Office supplied conservation images and helped edit Dr. Wolanin's chapter.

It was a special pleasure to collaborate with the Architect of the Capitol Photography Branch. Michael Dunn, chief of photography, provided a wealth of images, as well as his staff's time. Architectural photographer James Rosenthal's technical prowess and artistic grace greatly expanded the design possibilities of the book. The double spread on pages viii-ix showcases his photograph of the stately Brumidi Corridors. Overcoming the considerable optical and lighting challenges posed by the space, Mr. Rosenthal assembled a number of exposures into a single image that conveys the lofty feeling of standing at the barrel-vaulted corridors' cross point. No previous photograph or illustration has captured so effectively the gravitas of the monumental Brumidi Corridors and the union of Thomas U. Walter's architecture with Constantino Brumidi's painting.

The many fine professionals employed by the Government Printing Office turned the concept for a book on Brumidi into a finished product. Jessica Reynolds, visual information specialist, carried out the imaginative design and lavished attention on details large and small. With great patience and kindness, Sarah A. Wheeling, senior printing specialist, guided the preparation and production of the book, and she provided exceptional support throughout the lengthy and complex process. The expertise of Mary Ann Ullrich, assistant director of Congressional Publishing, enriched the book in a great many ways, and her enthusiasm and discerning eye were invaluable. I would like to thank Roger Jack, Sarah Jackson, and John Carey, printing services specialists with Quality Control, who provided helpful technical advice and guidance through the printing process. The efforts of Agency Publishing Services Team Two were also important in ensuring the quality of the printed book.

Over the years, the support and stewardship of congressional leaders have helped advance the programs necessary to safeguard and document the art of the U.S. Capitol for future generations. Special mention should be made to those who have cared for and have taken an interest in Constantino Brumidi's art since the artist completed his first fresco in 1855. The preservation and interpretation of Brumidi's historic works have been made possible by behind-the-scenes efforts of individuals, in all capacities and walks of life, both past and present. It is a privilege to work in this beautiful building, to care for its stately interiors, and to share Brumidi's heritage through this publication.

Amy Elizabeth Burton

About the Authors

Amy Elizabeth Burton is the assistant curator for the Office of Senate Curator. Ms. Burton earned her B.A. from Sweet Briar College and her M.A. in art history from Indiana University. She furthered her studies in art and architecture through programs in London and Florence. Specialized interests in ornithology and horticulture drive her current study of the flora and fauna depicted in the 19th-century murals of the Brumidi Corridors. Ms. Burton researches and writes for the office's publications, exhibits, and Web site. In 2009, she directed the documentary *Rediscovering an Historic Painting: Henry Clay in the U.S. Senate*, based on the extensive restoration of this Civil War-era painting.

Christiana Cunningham-Adams is an independent fine art paintings conservator who has lent her expertise in fresco conservation to the U.S. Capitol for two decades. After studying art history in Rome and graduating from the Istituto Centrale del Restauro in 1980, she completed an Advanced Painting Conservation internship at the Center for Conservation and Technical Studies at Harvard University's Fogg Art Museum in 1981. A fellow of the American Institute for Conservation of Historic and Artistic Works since 1993, and recipient of the National Trust for Historic Preservation Award in 2004, Ms. Cunningham-Adams has been the senior conservator and director of the Brumidi Corridors restoration project since 1991.

Donald A. Ritchie is the Senate historian and holds a Ph.D. in history from the University of Maryland. Dr. Ritchie is head of the Senate Historical Office, which provides information, pamphlets, articles, and books about Senate history for use by senators, staff, the media, scholars, and the general public. Dr. Ritchie has published a number of books, including *Press Gallery: Congress and the Washington Correspondents*, which won the Richard Leopold Prize from the Organization of American Historians; *Reporting from Washington: The History of the Washington Press Corp;* and *The U.S. Congress: A Very Short Introduction*.

Diane K. Skvarla became the Senate curator in 1995, having begun her career in the office in 1979. She directs the museum and preservation programs for the United States Senate under the authority of the Senate Commission on Art. The Curator's Office collects, preserves, and interprets the Senate's fine and decorative art, historic objects, and specific architectural features. Through exhibits, publications, and outreach programs, the office educates the public about the Senate and its collections. Ms. Skvarla has a B.A. in history from Colgate University and an M.A. in museum studies from The George Washington University. She co-authored the publications *United States Senate Catalogue of Fine Art* and *United States Senate Catalogue of Graphic Art*.

Barbara A. Wolanin has been the curator for the Architect of the Capitol since 1985. She is responsible for the art and historical records under the jurisdiction of the Architect and oversees the agency's art conservation program, recognized in 2010 by the American Institute for Conservation and Heritage Preservation. Dr. Wolanin prepared *Constantino Brumidi: Artist of the Capitol*, published for Congress in 1998. This book details Brumidi's 25-year career at the Capitol and highlights the conservation of his murals. Dr. Wolanin received a Ph.D. in art history from the University of Wisconsin in Madison and M.A. degrees from Harvard University and Oberlin College. She previously taught art history at the university level.

Opposite: **Squirrel clutching acorn, Brumidi Corridors (North Corridor).**

Notes

INTRODUCTION

1. "Death of a Great Artist," *Washington Post*, 20 February 1880.

2. *Congressional Record* (26 July 1951) vol. 97, pt. 14: A4712.

THE ENGINEER AND THE ARTIST

1. Montgomery C. Meigs, *Capitol Builder: The Shorthand Journals of Montgomery C. Meigs, 1853–1859, 1861*, edited by Wendy Wolff (Washington, D.C.: Government Printing Office, 2001), 748.

2. David W. Miller, *Second Only to Grant: Quartermaster General Montgomery C. Meigs: A Biography* (Shippensburg, PA: White Mane Books, 2000), 5.

3. Meigs, *Capitol Builder*, 349.

4. Miller, *Second Only to Grant*, 42.

5. Ibid., 30.

6. Ibid., 42.

7. Meigs, *Capitol Builder*, 179.

8. Ibid., 219–20.

9. Gordon S. Wood, *Empire of Liberty: A History of the Early Republic, 1789–1815* (New York: Oxford University Press, 2009), 553.

10. Meigs, *Capitol Builder*, 106.

11. Ibid., 180.

12. Ibid.

13. Ibid.

14. Ibid., 209.

15. Ibid., 222.

16. Ibid.

17. Ibid., 220.

18. Ibid., 223.

19. Ibid., 231.

20. Ibid., 232.

21. Ibid.

22. Ibid., 234.

23. Ibid., 235.

24. Ibid., 258.

25. Ibid., 258, 446.

26. Barbara A. Wolanin, *Constantino Brumidi: Artist of the Capitol* (Washington, D.C.: Government Printing Office, 1998), 64.

27. Ibid.

28. Charles E. Fairman, *Art and Artists of the Capitol of the United States of America* (Washington, D.C.: Government Printing Office, 1927), 161.

29. Wolanin, *Constantino Brumidi*, 70–71.

30. Meigs, *Capitol Builder*, 490.

31. Barbara A. Wolanin, "Meigs the Art Patron," in *Montgomery C. Meigs and the Building of the Nation's Capital*, edited by William C. Dickinson, Dean A. Herrin, and Donald R. Kennon (Athens, OH: Ohio University Press, 2001), 153.

32. Wolanin, *Constantino Brumidi*, 52.

33. Meigs, *Capitol Builder*, 497.

34. Ibid., 528.

35. Ibid.

36. "The Decoration of the Capitol," *New-York Daily Tribune*, 17 May 1858; Wolanin, "Meigs the Art Patron," in *Building of the Nation's Capital*, 162.

37. Wolanin, "Meigs the Art Patron," in *Building of the Nation's Capital*, 162.

38. Ibid., 163.

39. *Congressional Globe* (16 June 1860) 36th Cong., 1st sess.: 3045.

40. "The New Representatives' Hall," *Daily National Intelligencer*, 7 December 1857.

Opposite: **Compote with fruit and corn, Brumidi Corridors (North Corridor).**

41. Wolanin, *Constantino Brumidi*, 45.

42. Ibid., 91.

43. Meigs, *Capitol Builder*, 707.

44. Ibid., 774.

45. William C. Dickinson, "Montgomery C. Meigs, the New Age Public Manager: An Interpretive Essay," in *Montgomery C. Meigs and the Building of the Nation's Capital*, edited by William C. Dickinson, Dean A. Herrin, and Donald R. Kennon (Athens, OH: Ohio University Press, 2001), 168.

46. Wolanin, "Meigs the Art Patron," in *Building of the Nation's Capital*, 159.

47. Ibid., 160.

48. Ibid., 163.

49. Meigs, *Capitol Builder*, 511.

50. Wolanin, "Meigs the Art Patron," in *Building of the Nation's Capital*, 165.

THE UNLIKELY SIGNIFICANCE OF BRUMIDI'S MOTMOT

1. George Brown Goode, ed., *The Smithsonian Institution, 1846–1896. The History of Its First Half Century* (Washington, D.C.: n.p., 1897), 19–20.

2. E.F. Rivinus and E.M. Youssef, *Spencer Baird of the Smithsonian* (Washington, D.C.: Smithsonian Institution Press, 1992), 31.

3. E.F. Rivinus, "Spencer Fullerton Baird: The Collector of Collectors," *American Philatelist* 103, no. 11 (1989): 1062.

4. Richard G. Beidleman, *California's Frontier Naturalists* (Berkeley: University of California Press, 2006), 234.

5. Rivinus and Youssef, *Spencer Baird of the Smithsonian*, 63.

6. *Congressional Globe* (21 February 1861) 36th Cong., 2d sess.: 1088.

7. Ann Shelby Blum, *Picturing Nature: American Nineteenth-Century Zoological Illustration* (Princeton, NJ: Princeton University Press, 1993), 182.

8. DeB. Randolph Keim, *Keim's Illustrated Hand-Book. Washington and Its Environs: A Descriptive and Historical Hand-Book to the Capital of the United States of America* (Washington, D.C.: DeB. Randolph Keim, 1874), 52.

9. Montgomery C. Meigs, *Capitol Builder: The Shorthand Journals of Montgomery C. Meigs, 1853–1859, 1861*, edited by Wendy Wolff (Washington, D.C.: Government Printing Office, 2001), 106.

10. "The Decoration of the Capitol," *New-York Daily Tribune*, 17 May 1858.

11. *Congressional Record* (24 February 1880) vol. 10, pt. 2: 1075.

UNCOVERING THE HISTORIC ROOTS OF BRUMIDI'S DECORATIONS

1. Christiana Cunningham-Adams is an independent fine art paintings conservator working on the Brumidi Corridors restoration project under the auspices of the Architect of the Capitol.

THE "MOST PRACTICABLE" ROUTE

1. See Appendix B for the geographic locations of the scenes depicted in Brumidi's landscape medallions. As head painter, Brumidi is credited with the landscapes. He was responsible for the design of the murals in the Brumidi Corridors, and evidence suggests that he, rather than one of his assistant artists, painted the landscapes. Brumidi saved a number of preliminary oil studies of his work at the Capitol, including an oval landscape similar in style and shape to the Senate's medallions.

2. *Congressional Globe* (6 January 1859) 35th Cong., 2d sess.: 239.

3. Ibid., 240. At the time of Senator Harlan's speech on January 6, 1859, only 8 of the 12 volumes of the *Pacific Railroad Report* had been printed.

4. Alfred Frankenstein, "The Great Trans-Mississippi Railroad Survey," *Art in America* 64, no. 1 (January–February 1976): 56.

5. Montgomery C. Meigs, *Capitol Builder: The Shorthand Journals of Montgomery C. Meigs, 1853–1859, 1861*, edited by Wendy Wolff (Washington, D.C.: Government Printing Office, 2001), 443.

6. *Congressional Globe* (3 March 1853) 32nd Cong., 2d sess.: 1084.

7. David L. Nicandri, "The Romantic Western Narratives of the Artist John Mix Stanley," *Journal of American Culture* 9, no. 2 (summer 1986): 48.

8. U.S. House, *Reports of Explorations and Surveys, to Ascertain the Most Practicable and Economical Route for a Railroad from the Mississippi River to the Pacific Ocean*, vol. 12, 36th Cong., 1st sess., H. Exec. Doc. 56: 59.

9. Thomas S. Donaho, *Scenes and Incidents of Stanley's Western Wilds* (Washington, D.C.: Evening Star, 1854?), 8.

10. Robert Taft, "The Pictorial Record of the Old West: John M. Stanley and the Pacific Railroad Reports," *Kansas Historical Quarterly* 20, no. 1 (February 1952): 13.

11. U.S. Senate, *Reports of Explorations and Surveys, to Ascertain the Most Practicable and Economical Route for a Railroad from the Mississippi River to the Pacific Ocean*, vol. 2, 33rd Cong., 2d sess., S. Exec. Doc. 78: 75.

12. Ibid.

13. McDermott, Paul D., Ronald E. Grim, and Philip Mobley, *Eye of the Explorer: Views of the Northern Pacific Railroad Survey, 1853–54* (Missoula, Montana: Mountain Press Publishing, 2010), 3.

14. "Brumidi Paintings Found in Washington after a Search of Forty Years," *Washington, D.C. Star Sunday Magazine*, 2 November 1919, 6.

A COLLECTION OF BRUMIDI SKETCHES

1. Several publications discuss Meigs and his influence on the arts, including Lillian B. Miller, *Patrons and Patriotism: The Encouragement of the Fine Arts in the United States, 1790–1860* (Chicago: University of Chicago Press, 1966); Russell F. Weigley, "Captain Meigs and the Artists of the Capitol: Federal Patronage of Art in the 1850's," *Records of the Columbia Historical Society* 69–70 (1971): 285–305; Russell F. Weigley, *Quartermaster General of the Union Army: A Biography of M.C. Meigs* (New York: Columbia University Press, 1959); Barbara A. Wolanin, *Constantino Brumidi: Artist of the Capitol* (Washington, D.C.: Government Printing Office, 1998); and Barbara A. Wolanin, "Meigs the Art Patron," in *Montgomery C. Meigs and the Building of the Nation's Capital*, edited by William C. Dickinson, Dean A. Herrin, and Donald R. Kennon (Athens, OH: Ohio University Press, 2001), 133–65.

2. Montgomery C. Meigs to J. Durand, editor of *The Crayon*, October 11, 1856, Capitol Extension and New Dome Letterbooks, Records of the Architect of the Capitol.

3. Myrtle Cheney Murdock, *Constantino Brumidi: Michelangelo of the United States Capitol* (Washington, D.C.: Monumental, 1950), 6.

4. Wolanin, *Constantino Brumidi*, 53–59.

5. Ibid., 54.

6. Montgomery C. Meigs, *Capitol Builder: The Shorthand Journals of Montgomery C. Meigs, 1853–1859, 1861*, edited by Wendy Wolff (Washington, D.C.: Government Printing Office, 2001), 209.

7. Wolanin, *Constantino Brumidi,* 105–9.

8. Letter from artist Felix O.C. Darley sent by J. Durand to Montgomery C. Meigs, November 17, 1856, Architect of the Capitol, Curator's Office.

9. Francis V. O'Connor, "Constantino Brumidi as Decorator and History Painter: An Iconographic Analysis of Two Rooms in the United States Capitol," in *American Pantheon: Sculptural and Artistic Decoration of the United States Capitol*, edited by Donald R. Kennon and Thomas P. Somma (Athens, OH: Ohio University Press, 2004), 204–19.

10. Wolanin, *Constantino Brumidi*, 25–29.

11. *Congressional Record* (24 February 1880) vol. 10, pt. 2: 1075.

12. Meigs, *Capitol Builder*, 341.

13. Wolanin, *Constantino Brumidi*, 111–16.

14. Ibid., 224–29.

15. Ibid., 172; and "Brumidi Paintings Found in Washington after a Search of Forty Years," *Washington, D.C. Star Sunday Magazine*, 2 November 1919, 6.

16. Murdock, *Michelangelo of the United States Capitol*, 93.

17. Ibid.

18. Stephen Lake, e-mail message to author, October 4, 2010.

19. "Brumidi's Life Work," *Washington Post*, 11 April 1879.

20. Ibid.

21. "Death of a Great Artist," *Washington Post*, 20 February 1880.

22. "Brumidi's Life Work," *Washington Post*, 11 April 1879.

CONTINUING CONSERVATION OF BRUMIDI'S MURALS

1. The conservation program at the Capitol began with a comprehensive survey of the murals. Bernard Rabin and Constance S. Silver, "Conservation of Mural Paintings in the Capitol Building: Report on a Preliminary Study Carried out on January 21–22, 1981," March 17, 1981, Records of the Architect of the Capitol.

2. *Constantino Brumidi: Artist of the Capitol* was prepared under the direction of the Architect of the Capitol for Congress. Barbara A. Wolanin, *Constantino Brumidi: Artist of the Capitol* (Washington, D.C.: Government Printing Office, 1998).

3. Wolanin, *Constantino Brumidi*, 54–59.

4. Bernard Rabin and Constance S. Silver, Rabin and Krueger Paintings, "U.S. Capitol Building Room H–144 Conservation of Mural Paintings," December 12, 1988; Arthur Page, Page Conservation, Inc., "Conservation of H–144 Walls," February 28, 2005, Records of the Architect of the Capitol.

5. Quoted in "The Decoration of the Capitol," *New-York Daily Tribune*, 17 May 1858. See also Wolanin, *Constantino Brumidi*, 69. What Brumidi knew as the Baths of Titus was actually Emperor Nero's Golden Palace buried beneath the later baths.

6. Wolanin, *Constantino Brumidi*, 68–69.

7. Barbara Ramsay, ARTEX Fine Arts Services, "Preliminary Condition Assessment of the Brumidi Murals, U.S. Capitol, Senate Appropriations Committee Hearing Room," November 3, 2003, Records of the Architect of the Capitol.

8. Barbara Ramsay, ARTEX Fine Arts Services, Conservation treatment reports for Senate Appropriations Committee Hearing Room, S–127, March 2004; February 2005; December 6, 2010; and March 31, 2012, Records of the Architect of the Capitol.

9. In 1959, five portraits of notable senators were added to fill the ovals on the Senate Reception Room walls: *John C. Calhoun* by Arthur E. Schmalz Conrad; *Henry Clay* by Allyn Cox; *Daniel Webster* by Adrian S. Lamb; *Robert A. Taft* by Deane Keller; and *Robert M. La Follette* by Robert Chester La Follette. Three of the lunettes' rondels were filled in the 21st century: *Arthur H. Vandenberg* by Michael Shane Neal, 2004; *Robert F. Wagner* by Steven Polson, 2004; and *The Connecticut Compromise* by Bradley Stevens, 2006.

10. Constance S. Silver, Preservar, Inc., "U.S. Capitol Building, Senate Reception Room: Report on the Ongoing Treatment of the Art and Finishes," May 12, 1995; and "The Conservation Treatment of Room S–213, The Senate Reception Room, U.S. Capitol Building," March 1997, Records of the Architect of the Capitol.

11. William A. Lewin and Davida Kovner, William A. Lewin Conservator LLC, "Analysis Report: Gilded Wall Surfaces in the U.S. Senate Reception Room, S–213," May 23, 2011; "Conservation Research Report," September 30, 2011; and "Phase II Pilot Conservation Treatment Report: Senate Reception Room S–213," November 30, 2011, Records of the Architect of the Capitol.

12. Laurie A. Timm, "Senate Reception Room Lunettes S–213: Plaster Consolidation and Overpaint Removal/ Adjustment," April 28, 2011, Records of the Architect of the Capitol.

13. Montgomery C. Meigs, *Capitol Builder: The Shorthand Journals of Montgomery C. Meigs, 1853–1859, 1861*, edited by Wendy Wolff (Washington, D.C.: Government Printing Office, 2001), 106; Giovanni Volpato and Giovanni Ottaviani, *Loggie di Rafaele nel Vaticano* (Rome: n.p., 1772–77).

14. Will Yandik, "The Birds of the Brumidi Corridors," *The Capitol Dome*, 40, no. 3 (summer 2003): 3–5; Jamie Whitacre, "The Fruits and Flowers of the Brumidi Corridors," *The Capitol Dome*, 44, no. 2 (spring 2007): 9–14.

15. Arthur Page, Page Conservation, Inc., "2002 Preliminary Study: Condition Assessment and Recommended Treatment for Untreated Sections of the Senate Brumidi Corridors of the U.S. Capitol," November 5, 2002; Christiana Cunningham-Adams, Cunningham-Adams Conservation, "Conservation Treatment and Research Report: Investigation, Testing, and Analysis for Completion of the Brumidi Corridors Restoration," November 15, 2010, Records of the Architect of the Capitol.

16. Christiana Cunningham-Adams and George Adams, Cunningham-Adams Fine Arts Painting Conservation, "Brumidi Corridors Restoration Plan," January 4, 1994; and additional Brumidi Corridors conservation treatment reports by Cunningham-Adams, "Phase I," November 1, 1997; "Phase II," April 10, 1998; "Phase III," March 8, 1999; "Phase IV," December 14, 2001; "Phase V," August 27, 2001; "Phase VI," July 14, 2003; "Phase VII," November 24, 2003; "Phase VIII," January 13, 2005; "Phase IX," May 31, 2007; "Phase X," May 30, 2008; and "Phase XI," November 30, 2009, Records of the Architect of the Capitol.

17. Christiana Cunningham-Adams, Cunningham-Adams Fine Arts Painting Conservation, "U.S. Senate North Entrance Murals, Brumidi Corridors Restoration Phase XI," November 30, 2009, Records of the Architect of the Capitol.

18. As president pro tempore and chairman of the Appropriations Committee, Senator Daniel K. Inouye of Hawaii was instrumental in the effort to remove the temporary wall and to reintegrate the space with the corridor system. Regrettably, Senator Inouye died before the wall was removed and the conservation of the Zodiac Corridor completed.

19. Christiana Cunningham-Adams, Cunningham-Adams Conservation, "Zodiac Corridor Restoration, vol.1: Ceiling Decoration, vol. 2: Wall Paintings," June 20, 2013, Records of the Architect of the Capitol.

20. Christiana Cunningham-Adams, Cunningham-Adams Conservation, "Conservation Treatment Report: Trophy Room Painted Ceiling and Four Lunettes in U.S. Capitol," October 3, 2011; and "Restoration Treatment Report: Trophy Rooms Walls and Refectory Area Walls," January 2103, Records of the Architect of the Capitol.

21. *An Act to award posthumously a Congressional gold medal to Constantino Brumidi*, Public Law 110–259, 122 Stat. 2431 (2008): 2–3.

Selected Bibliography

INTRODUCTION

"Death of a Great Artist," *Washington Post*, 20 February 1880.

U.S. House. Representative Victor L. Anfuso of Kentucky speaking on the 146th anniversary of the birth of Constantino Brumidi. *Congressional Record* (26 July 1951) vol. 97, pt. 14.

THE ENGINEER AND THE ARTIST

"The Decoration of the Capitol," *New-York Daily Tribune*, 17 May 1858.

Dickinson, William C., Dean A. Herrin, and Donald R. Kennon, eds. *Montgomery C. Meigs and the Building of the Nation's Capital*. Athens, OH: Ohio University Press, 2001.

Fairman, Charles E. *Art and Artists of the Capitol of the United States of America*. Washington, D.C.: Government Printing Office, 1927.

Fryd, Vivien Green. *Art and Empire: The Politics of Ethnicity in the United States Capitol, 1815–1860*. New Haven, CT: Yale University Press, 1992.

Kennon, Donald R., and Thomas P. Somma, eds. *American Pantheon: Sculptural and Artistic Decoration of the United States Capitol*. Athens, OH: Ohio University Press, 2004.

Meigs, Montgomery C. *Capitol Builder: The Shorthand Journals of Montgomery C. Meigs, 1853–1859, 1861*. Edited by Wendy Wolff. Washington, D.C.: Government Printing Office, 2001.

Miller, David W. *Second Only to Grant: Quartermaster General Montgomery C. Meigs: A Biography*. Shippensburg, PA: White Mane Books, 2000.

"The New Representatives' Hall," *Daily National Intelligencer*, 7 December 1857.

U.S. House. Representative John Cochrane of New York speaking on the decoration of the Capitol. *Congressional Globe* (16 June 1860) 36th Cong., 1st sess.

Wolanin, Barbara A. *Constantino Brumidi: Artist of the Capitol*. Washington, D.C.: Government Printing Office, 1998.

Wood, Gordon S. *Empire of Liberty: A History of the Early Republic, 1789–1815*. New York: Oxford University Press, 2009.

THE UNLIKELY SIGNIFICANCE OF BRUMIDI'S MOTMOT

Beidleman, Richard G. *California's Frontier Naturalists*. Berkeley: University of California Press, 2006.

Blum, Ann Shelby. *Picturing Nature: American Nineteenth-Century Zoological Illustration*. Princeton, NJ: Princeton University Press, 1993.

"The Decoration of the Capitol," *New-York Daily Tribune*, 17 May 1858.

Goode, George Brown, ed. *The Smithsonian Institution, 1846–1896. The History of Its First Half Century*. Washington, D.C.: n.p., 1897.

Keim, DeB. Randolph. *Keim's Illustrated Hand-Book. Washington and Its Environs: A Descriptive and Historical Hand-Book to the Capital of the United States of America*. Washington, D.C.: DeB. Randolph Keim, 1874.

Meigs, Montgomery C. *Capitol Builder: The Shorthand Journals of Montgomery C. Meigs, 1853–1859, 1861*. Edited by Wendy Wolff. Washington, D.C.: Government Printing Office, 2001.

Rhees, William Jones, ed. *The Smithsonian Institution: Documents Relative to Its Origin and History*. Vol. 17. Washington, D.C.: Smithsonian Institution, 1880.

Rivinus, E.F. "Spencer Fullerton Baird: The Collector of Collectors." *American Philatelist* 103, no. 11 (1989).

Rivinus, E.F., and E.M. Youssef. *Spencer Baird of the Smithsonian*. Washington, D.C.: Smithsonian Institution Press, 1992.

U.S. Senate. *Report on the United States and Mexican Boundary Survey*, 3 vols., 34th Cong., 1st sess., S. Exec. Doc. 108.

———. *Reports of Explorations and Surveys, to Ascertain the Most Practicable and Economical Route for a Railroad from the Mississippi River to the Pacific Ocean*, 11 vols., 33rd Cong., 2d sess., S. Exec. Doc. 78; and vol. 12, 35th Cong., 2d sess., S. Exec. Doc. 46.

Opposite: **History and Father Time,** detail from *History,* fresco, **1867.**

U.S. Senate. Senator Daniel Voorhees of Indiana speaking in eulogy on the late Constantino Brumidi. *Congressional Record* (24 February 1880) vol. 10, pt. 2.

U.S. Senate. Senator Simon Cameron of Pennsylvania speaking on appropriations to fund scientific expeditions. *Congressional Globe* (21 February 1861) 36th Cong., 2d sess.

Viola, Herman J. *Exploring the West.* Washington, D.C.: Smithsonian Institution Press, 1987.

Viola, Herman J. and Carolyn Margolis, eds. *Magnificent Voyagers: The U.S. Exploring Expedition, 1838–1842.* Washington, D.C.: Smithsonian Institution Press, 1985.

THE "MOST PRACTICABLE" ROUTE

Bedell, Rebecca. *The Anatomy of Nature: Geology and American Landscape Painting, 1825–1875.* Princeton, NJ: Princeton University Press, 2001.

Billington, David P. *The Innovators: The Engineering Pioneers Who Made America Modern.* New York: John Wiley and Sons, 1996.

"Brumidi Paintings Found in Washington after a Search of Forty Years." *Washington, D.C. Star Sunday Magazine,* 2 November 1919.

Donaho, Thomas S. *Scenes and Incidents of Stanley's Western Wilds.* Washington, D.C.: Evening Star, n.d., ca. 1854.

Frankenstein, Alfred. "The Great Trans-Mississippi Railroad Survey." *Art in America* 64, no.1 (January–February 1976).

Goetzmann, William H. *Army Exploration in the American West, 1803–1863.* Austin: Texas State Historical Association, 1991.

McDermott, Paul D., Ronald E. Grim, and Philip Mobley. *Eye of the Explorer: Views of the Northern Pacific Railroad Survey, 1853–54.* Missoula, Montana: Mountain Press Publishing, 2010.

Meigs, Montgomery C. *Capitol Builder: The Shorthand Journals of Montgomery C. Meigs, 1853–1859, 1861.* Edited by Wendy Wolff. Washington, D.C.: Government Printing Office, 2001.

Nicandri, David L. "The Romantic Western Narratives of the Artist John Mix Stanley." *Journal of American Culture* 9, no. 2 (summer 1986).

Novak, Barbara. *Nature and Culture: American Landscape and Painting, 1825–1875.* New York: Oxford University Press, 2007.

Taft, Robert. *Artists and Illustrators of the Old West, 1850–1900.* New York: Charles Scribner's Sons, 1953.

———. "The Pictorial Record of the Old West: John M. Stanley and the Pacific Railroad Reports." *Kansas Historical Quarterly* 20, no. 1 (February 1952).

Thomas, William G. *The Iron Way: Railroads, the Civil War, and the Making of Modern America.* New Haven, CT: Yale University Press, 2011.

U.S. House. *Reports of Explorations and Surveys, to Ascertain the Most Practicable and Economical Route for a Railroad from the Mississippi River to the Pacific Ocean,* 11 vols., 33rd Cong., 2d sess., H. Exec. Doc. 91; and vol. 12, 36th Cong., 1st sess., H. Exec. Doc. 56.

U.S. Senate. Indian Appropriation Bill. *Congressional Globe* (3 March 1853) 32nd Cong., 2d sess.

———. *Reports of Explorations and Surveys, to Ascertain the Most Practicable and Economical Route for a Railroad from the Mississippi River to the Pacific Ocean,* 11 vols., 33rd Cong., 2d sess., S. Exec. Doc. 78; and vol. 12, 35th Cong., 2d sess., S. Exec. Doc. 46.

———. Senator James Harlan of Iowa speaking on the Pacific Railroad. *Congressional Globe* (6 January 1859) 35th Cong., 2d sess.

A COLLECTION OF BRUMIDI SKETCHES

"Brumidi Paintings Found in Washington after a Search of Forty Years." *Washington, D.C. Star Sunday Magazine,* 2 November 1919.

"Brumidi's Life Work," *Washington Post,* 11 April 1879.

"Death of a Great Artist," *Washington Post,* 20 February 1880.

Meigs, Montgomery C. *Capitol Builder: The Shorthand Journals of Montgomery C. Meigs, 1853–1859, 1861.* Edited by Wendy Wolff. Washington, D.C.: Government Printing Office, 2001.

Miller, Lillian B. *Patrons and Patriotism: The Encouragement of the Fine Arts in the United States, 1790–1860.* Chicago: University of Chicago Press, 1966.

Murdock, Myrtle Cheney. *Constantino Brumidi: Michelangelo of the United States Capitol.* Washington, D.C.: Monumental, 1950.

O'Connor, Francis V. "Constantino Brumidi as Decorator and History Painter: An Iconographic Analysis of Two Rooms in the United States Capitol." In *American Pantheon: Sculptural and Artistic Decoration of the United States Capitol,* edited by Donald R. Kennon and Thomas P. Somma. Athens, OH: Ohio University Press, 2004.

U.S. Senate. Senator Daniel Voorhees of Indiana speaking in eulogy on the late Constantino Brumidi. *Congressional Record* (24 February 1880) vol. 10, pt. 2.

Weigley, Russell F. "Captain Meigs and the Artists of the Capitol: Federal Patronage of Art in the 1850's." *Records of the Columbia Historical Society* 69–70 (1971).

———. *Quartermaster General of the Union Army: A Biography of M.C. Meigs.* New York: Columbia University Press, 1959.

Wolanin, Barbara A. *Constantino Brumidi: Artist of the Capitol.* Washington, D.C.: Government Printing Office, 1998.

Wolanin, Barbara A. "Meigs the Art Patron." In *Montgomery C. Meigs and the Building of the Nation's Capital,* edited by William C. Dickinson, Dean A. Herrin, and Donald R. Kennon. Athens, OH: Ohio University Press, 2001.

CONTINUING CONSERVATION OF BRUMIDI'S MURALS

"The Decoration of the Capitol," *New-York Daily Tribune,* 17 May 1858.

Meigs, Montgomery C. *Capitol Builder: The Shorthand Journals of Montgomery C. Meigs, 1853–1859, 1861.* Edited by Wendy Wolff. Washington, D.C.: Government Printing Office, 2001.

Whitacre, Jamie. "The Fruits and Flowers of the Brumidi Corridors." *The Capitol Dome* 44, no. 2 (spring 2007).

Wolanin, Barbara A. *Constantino Brumidi: Artist of the Capitol.* Washington, D.C.: Government Printing Office, 1998.

Yandik, Will. "The Birds of the Brumidi Corridors." *The Capitol Dome* 40, no. 3 (summer 2003).

Photography Credits

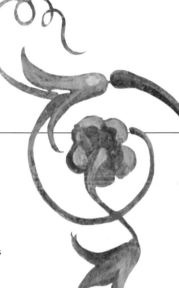

Principal photography was provided by James Rosenthal, courtesy of the Architect of the Capitol. Room views and other illustrations photographed by Mr. Rosenthal in 2013 are noted below.

Cover; full page view of North and West Corridors, pages viii–ix; full page view of President's Room, page 5; full page view of Senate Appropriations Committee Room, page 10; Brumidi Corridors' murals, pages 26–29, 34, and 41 (image on right); full page view of Senate reception area, page 47; conservation exposure tests, pages 48 and 49; conservator at work, page 50; Brumidi Corridors' murals, page 51; landscape medallions conserved in 2013, pages 52, 54, 55, 57, 60, 61, 64, and 66; *Liberty, Peace, Plenty, War,* page 67; *Death of General Wooster, 1777,* page 77; full page view of Senate Reception Room (during conservation of walls), page 80; Senate Appropriations Committee Room mural, page 86; Senate Appropriations Committee Room, page 90 (image on right); full page view of Senate Reception Room, page 97; Webster portrait panel, page 98 (image on right); Zodiac Corridor ceiling, page 103 (image at bottom); full page view of Zodiac Corridor, page 105; full page detail of bronze railing, page 110; full page detail of North Corridor mural, page 120; full page detail from President's Room, page 130.

Additional photographs, including those listed below, were provided from the records of the Architect of the Capitol Photography Branch.

Charles Badal: *Calling of Putnam from the Plow to the Revolution,* page 9; full page view of Rotunda, page 17; House Agriculture Committee Room, page 88; Senate Reception Room, page 96; conservators at work, page 99 (image at top and lower right); Zodiac Corridor ceiling, page 103 (image at top); Zodiac Corridor mural, page 104 (image at top); Trophy Room, page 107 (image at top); Constantino Brumidi Congressional Gold Medal, page 109.

Susanne Bledsoe: West Corridor panel, page 30.

Wayne Firth: *Thomas Ustick Walter,* page 6; *Calling of Cincinnatus from the Plow,* page 8 (image at bottom); *Cornwallis Sues for Cessation of Hostilities under the Flag of Truce,* page 14; *The Apotheosis of Washington,* page 16; full page detail of *History,* page 126.

Conservation images are from the records of the Architect of the Capitol. Photographic support for images in the collection of the Office of Senate Curator was provided by the Sergeant at Arms Senate Photo Studio and Government Printing Office.

Architect of the Capitol

Opposite: Trompe l'oeil mural by Brumidi, with gilded mirror frame and curtain tieback in the foreground, President's Room.

2015